"In her book, The Red Thread, Lucinda Smith uncovers God's longings for us and draws us to find freedom, identity, and wholeness in our Heavenly Father. Her story of hope will inspire a new and fearless hope within you, and stir you to reach out with honesty to our loving Father amidst any and all circumstances."

ERIC SANDOR – *Author, Speaker and Trustee of David's Tent*

"Here's a very honest book about how we can be freed from the crippling emotions of defeat, disappointment and dispaiar. Lucinda's story turns the reader's attention to Jesus and how being in relationship with Him will bring hope forgiveness, peace and adoption into his family. The powerful chapter on the devil is certainly one which Satan would not want us to read!"

RT REV JULIAN HENDERSON – *Bishop of Blackburn*

"The Red Thread goes straight for the heart and the reader can't run away from the reality that God is our Father and He is building a family of sons and daughters. Lucinda is a guide not just a writer, pulling all of her words from experience that she has lived. It's the Lucinda's of this world that move the bride closer to the bridegroom."

JONATHAN HORSFALL – *Pastor, Life Church Bath*

THE RED THREAD

LUCINDA SMITH

Published by Live From Rest Publications
www.livefromrest.com
lucinda@livefromrest.com

Published March 2022
Copyright © 2022 Lucinda Smith

CONTENTS

CONTENTS

I dedicate this book to
Phoebe Kaijuan Smith –
your beautiful story continues
to speak to me today.

THANK YOU

To Paul at Zaccmedia for your help and advice.

To Josh for encouraging me to write this book,
and for believing in me.

To Steve for endless hours of tech support and
for the gift of a desk and computer that kick
started the writing!

To the dear friends who have walked with me,
prayed with me and cheered me on
these past few years.

PREFACE

I never intended to write a book. It simply began to write itself. I am not like some, compelled to jot down thoughts and ideas and scribblings in a little notebook (or perhaps more accurately, a phone!). I once wrote some poetry – a long time ago – but, for some reason or another, never did so again.

I am a mother, grandmother, sister, wife, friend, aunty, like billions of others. When I first met Jesus, I had plans to change the world for Him. Well, not quite. But certainly, a little piece of it. With my nursing qualification firmly tucked under my belt, I would be off, or so I thought.

Nothing has worked out quite the way I had hoped it would. For so very long I felt as if I never quite knew what it was that

God had uniquely put in me – I had never quite experienced the *'this* is why God has put me here' moment. Not that I haven't enjoyed many, many wonderful moments, but I think some of you understand what I mean.

Our stint in Pakistan as medical missionaries left me feeling all the more confused and bewildered and lost. That was the only thing I had really, really wanted to do, and yet it felt as though we returned home to the UK with our tail between our legs, after only six short years. We had signed up for life – told God we were in it for the long haul.

I look back over the years and I see lots of frustration and disappointment in unfulfilled dreams, but I also recognise something deep and rich that has been slowly evolving in my heart. The finger of God has been tenderly drawing me into completeness and healing.

So, this is why I write this book – that my identity journey might encourage you, in yours. My desire is that you will find wholeness and freedom in discovering who you were created to be and in recognising who it is who keeps and sustains you. For you see, we are all broken and damaged – we are all cracked vessels. Since the Garden of Eden days, we have all been searching for that which will complete us. Some of us have been more honest than others in acknowledging our lack and our loss, but even those of us who, in encountering God, hoped for fullness – we too know we aren't who we could be, who we want to be.

I really want you to see that while good theology and head knowledge has its place and is important, it is in your heart that you will truly meet and know God. We can all say the right things, play the part, look like the person we aspire to be. But it is the state of our heart that He sees. This book is an attempt, on my behalf, to tempt you to be open before the One who beckons you and pursues you and longs for you, so that in your vulnerability you might know Him all the more intimately.

I pray that you will be brave and courageous – that you will take the risk, be honest before Him and allow Him into your secret places. In His sight you are worthy of all that He offers you, but perhaps you have not yet truly begun to plumb the depths of His extravagant love and extraordinary goodness that awaits you, wherever you are currently on this journey to **true identity**.

God bless you richly!

INTRODUCTION

She was very small with hair as fine and wispy as air itself. She held her shoes very tightly, clinging on for dear life to the only possessions she had! And they looked new, as though they had never been worn. Her distress was obvious – she was clinging like a little limpet to the man. We had to peel her away from him, but this was a good sign – she had been attached to someone and would hopefully bond again.

'The long red thread' that had wound its way from Southern China to our home in West Yorkshire had been diminishing in length as the months passed. As the imminence of our meeting approached, the future of this little girl and her connection to our family pulled us closer, until now, in that place, in Nanning,

Guangxi province, our lives became entwined. [1]There is an old Chinese proverb that says a red thread connects those who are destined to be together and so it was that there, in that moment, God's plan for our family to embrace and envelope this little one, was being realised.

We adopted Phoebe over 16 years ago now, and it has been one of the most wonderful things we have ever done. She is a joy and a delight, and God has shown me many things that I perhaps could not have understood, had we not lived through our adoption story.

I did not know it was possible to fiercely love another's child. I did not know it was possible to care so deeply and so totally about someone from another race and culture. I did not know that I could make sacrifices for this one, as I had done for the three children born of my own flesh and blood. I did not know that my heart would sometimes break and that I would weep over her loss of culture, identity, family.

I see now that there truly is a 'blood' red thread of divine connection, sometimes tenuous and worn thin, sometimes strong and robust, that winds itself around the earth, crisscrossing cultures and traditions, belief systems and values, connecting every heart upon this planet to the heart of God, our Abba, Father.

---

1   This ancient Chinese proverb finds a Biblical echo in Paul's letter to the Ephesian church. There we read 'even as he chose us in him before the foundation of the world, that we should be holy and blameless before him. In love he predestined us for adoption to himself as sons through Jesus Christ, according to the purpose of his will' (Ephesians 1:4,5).

1

SO, WHO IS GOD?

'But what about you?' he asked. 'Who do you say I am?'
JESUS CHRIST

About 20 years ago, you would have found me crippled with insecurities, unable to see through the fog that was clinical depression. Some of you may know what that feels like. It is horrible. I was in the pit. I had a lot of anger; a sense of abandonment enveloped me, and I was dogged by a plethora of emotions that I couldn't make sense of.

On becoming followers of Jesus, many of us, at that very point, did receive a big measure of tangible freedom. Some people say that they inexplicably and quite suddenly stopped swearing or were able to effortlessly give up smoking. We had a sense of peace that perhaps had always eluded us. We had been transferred from the kingdom of darkness into the kingdom of light, whether we were aware of that or not. This is *huge*. But there is a verse in Paul's letter to the Galatians that also suggests a second freedom:

> It is for freedom that Christ has set us free. Stand firm, then, and do not let yourselves be burdened again by a yoke of slavery.
>
> (Galatians 5:1)

It is for *freedom* that we've been set free. So, what is this second freedom? And how is it linked to our theme of identity?

The freedom referred to is not dancing at the back of church or raising your hands in worship. This second freedom is far more profound. In my experience of teaching and mentoring young women, and from years of one-to-one deeper prayer ministry, I know that an increasing number of Christians are finding themselves crippled by low self-esteem, by insecurities, by anxiety, by depression, by fear. These prevent them from stepping into the destiny that God has for them. These strong, often life-controlling emotions hold us all back, in one way or another, from being the people God created us to be.

Me, for example, I was Bible-believing, born again, Spirit-filled, and yet far from experiencing freedom. Clearly, I had submitted again to a yoke of slavery. But how had that happened?

It's my belief that unless we truly understand who God really is, who we are and who our enemy is, from a Biblical perspective, we will *never* be free. In those hard, hard years I did not know what I now know to be true, and if I had known, perhaps my life today would look quite different.

I want you to know that there is real hope for you that this freedom can be a reality in your life. I felt overlooked, misunderstood, undervalued and betrayed and, on top of those feelings, I was trying to cope with living in a Muslim country. I was completely paralysed, with no hope at all. What I wanted then, of course, is different from what you're wanting; the hopes that you have now are not the same as those that I had, and they're not the same as the next person's. But we all have hopes. We all have dreams.

We sometimes use this beautiful word, 'hope' very lightly. 'I hope they have it in my size,' we might remark. But then, we also use it when things matter very much indeed. 'I hope he doesn't die,' we weep. I wonder what we really mean when we use the word 'hope'?

I believe that for those of us who know God, this little word needs to mean something different from what it means to those who don't know Him.

The Oxford English dictionary says that 'to hope' means 'to want something to happen or be the case'. I think we all do, in fact, use the word 'hope' with this definition somewhere in the back of our mind. But there is a huge difference between how the world uses the word and how followers of Jesus should understand it and use it.

You see, when the world uses it, there's an element of doubt.

'Hope' is commonly used to mean a wish. Its strength, you could say, lies in the depth and firmness of the person's desire. But in the Bible, hope is the confident expectation of what God has promised, and its strength is in His nature, in who He says He is and indeed *is*!

It is interesting that in the Old Testament the Hebrew word for hope, *batah*, and its cognates has the meaning of confidence, security, and being without care. Therefore, the concept of doubt is not part of this word.

Likewise, in most instances in the New Testament, the word 'hope' is the Greek *elpis/elpizo*. Again, there is no doubt attached to this word. Biblical hope is therefore a confident expectation or assurance based upon a sure foundation for which we wait with joy and full confidence. In other words, there is no doubt about it!

About ten years ago Steve, my husband, quoted to me from a book he was reading by the well-known Christian author Francis Frangipane, and it said something akin to 'Unless you have glistening hope in every area of your life, you are believing a lie.'

I screamed at him, 'That's not true! There is no hope that this situation could ever be different!' I was incensed and seriously offended at such a suggestion.

Now, all these years later, I completely agree with Francis Frangipane's statement, and the story of how I got from there to here is the basis of this book.

When people who don't know Jesus use the word 'hope', it might, in some cases, be based on the moral character of a person. Hoping for a job promotion, for example, depends on the boss, whether he likes you or not, thinks you're competent or not, thinks you're right for the job – whether he can get you to work longer hours than what he pays you for, perhaps! Or hope, in the worldly sense, might depend on more random circumstances, such as the weather or the traffic or the housing market or the stock exchange. It's all a bit arbitrary.

When we were in Pakistan, at my lowest, and in the darkest of places – I certainly had no hope – Steve couldn't fix me. I couldn't fix me. Being a missionary, fulfilling what I thought was my dream, didn't seem to be the answer either.

But our hope as Christians is based on the nature of God.

With this in mind, we can confidently and legitimately hope that our dreams and desires will come to pass, but if they don't, then there is an equally confident expectation that however it pans out, it will be good, it will be better than OK. It may not be what we want or what we dreamed or planned, or what we expected, but it will be good because that hope is based on the nature of God, and the nature of God is good. *Always good.*

Psalm 62:5–6 says this:

> Yes, my soul, find rest in God;
>   my hope comes from him.
> Truly he is my rock and my salvation;
>   he is my fortress, I shall not be shaken.

But what happens if God is not your rock? What if He is not really that trustworthy, you cannot quite depend on Him in this situation – you are not 100% sure that He cares, sees, knows *you*?

God promises to turn all things around for our good. This means even tragedies. Romans 8:28 says: 'we know that in all things God works for the good of those who love him, who have been called according to his purpose.' So even if, or should I say *when*, things go wrong, God promises to turn things around for our highest good and for His greatest glory. I now believe that it is absolutely possible to have joy, peace and *hope*, and live free from anxiety and fear, no matter what life throws at us, no matter what the newspaper says, no matter how 'scary' Covid-19 seems to be.

However, I have not always been able to live from this standpoint, and how I arrived here is my story. I had hoped to have been a long-term missionary, but after six years in Pakistan we came home to the UK defeated, and for many years I didn't allow myself to hope for anything much. I had had too many disappointments; too many broken dreams lay in pieces at my feet. But, in those days, I didn't know the nature of God – the true Biblical character of God, as He defines Himself.

To live daily with a modicum of this glorious hope, we must know who God is. What is He really like? And can we truly trust Him?

We live in a world surrounded by disaster, pain and injustice. The earth itself is bearing scars and suffering wounds, inflicted upon it by our greed and complacency and ignorance. More human beings than ever before are enslaved or trafficked or living with abuse and violence. In our despair it would be so easy for us all, and indeed it is for many, to give up all hope for a bright future. However, as followers of Jesus, we can have hope because it is possible to know God. It is not that we know Him according to *our* idea of what He is like, but rather we can know Him according to who *He* says He is.

If the picture of God that you have in your mind is even slightly off centre, if it is even minutely skew-whiff, then you can be sure that this inaccuracy about the nature of God will one day get you into trouble. At some point we have to choose to believe who God says He is, *not* who we think He is. Coming to grips with this fact has totally changed me, it has changed my relationship with God, and ultimately it has resulted in me being able to live 80% of the time in peace and contentment. Yes, I have my down days; yes, I sometimes rant and rave; and no, I do not understand why things happen to me. Yes, life seems so unfair sometimes, and it's hard to be misunderstood or wrongly judged, *but* knowing without a shadow of a doubt that *God is good*, always good, makes all the difference, and means that I can experience peace in the middle of the stuff of life.

Let me ask you a question. Do you believe that the Bible is God's word? By this I'm not asking whether you believe that every story happened exactly as you read it, word for word; it's more about the things that God says to us and about us, the references He makes to Himself in relation to us. I think many of you reading this will be nodding your heads, and saying 'Yes, yes, I do believe that it is God's word!' But if I said to you, 'Do you have glistening hope in every area of your life?', what would you say? That is, in your health, in your finances, work, family, church relationships, for your dreams? Is your answer still a resounding 'yes'? I imagine most of us, perhaps even all, would at this point have to answer 'no'. 'No, there really is no hope that this area of my life might change, that that particular situation could ever improve, that my dreams could one day be fulfilled.'

So, there is a disconnect. On the one hand we are willing to talk and sing about God being all these wonderful things – good, faithful, our provider, our healer, our protector – and yes, we say that we believe that the Bible speaks God's words, and yet on the other hand we do not have glistening hope in every area of our lives.

Let's take fear for a moment. Fear robs us of hope because, simply put, it is the future without God. Think about it for a moment. Fear is the thought or anticipation of a future event, whether that is going to the dentist in an hour, or the possibility of a cancer diagnosis one day, without the presence of God – in our minds and hearts we have not invited God into it. We are not envisioning Him there. We have left Him behind. He does not feature. If He did, would we still be fearful? The readiness with which we fear displays greater faith in the devil's ability to harm us than in God's ability to protect, provide, heal, lead, guide or sustain us. 'Do not fear' is written 365 times in the Bible. Once for every day of the year! Surely, that is telling. Yet many, many Christians are fearful. I think we have a problem, and I believe it is this: we don't take His word seriously. We don't, really believe God when He speaks.

I totally understand how this happens because it happened to me. I absolutely understand how it happens, but I also know that it is possible to stop it from happening. We can live from a place of victory, in peace, free from fear and anxiety. *But* we have to really want this freedom, and we will need to make some choices, as I had to.

So, having looked at the promise of freedom in Galatians chapter 5, and having discussed Biblical hope based on the revealed nature of God, let's get back to the title of this chapter: 'So, who is God?'

The well-loved theologian and author A. W. Tozer once said this: 'What comes into our minds when we think about God is the most important thing about us.'[2] He is, of course, absolutely right because this image of God, whether held by a follower of Jesus or by an atheist, affects everything. It determines everything: what you look like out there in the workplace, in the marketplace, with your family and friends; how you make decisions; how you confront evil; what you do with disappointment, sadness, loss, grief, joy. If the image in your mind is correct, based on the Biblical revelation of the nature of God, you won't take offence, you won't mind if others are promoted over you, you won't compare yourself to others, you won't strive for praise and approval, you won't be jealous of other people's success. You can even afford to fail and mess up because He will be your joy, and in Him you will continue to place your hope. He will be that fortress you run to when everything else is unstable, and what He says about you will be all that counts.

> Yes, my soul, find rest in God;
> *my hope comes from him.*
> Truly he is my rock and my salvation;
>   he is my fortress, I will not be shaken.
>
> (Psalm 62:5–6, italics mine)

Just take a moment to imagine the phenomenal impact the people of God could have on our communities, if we all lived with an image of God in our heads and in our hearts that was in perfect tune with the revelation that God Himself gives of His nature. There would be no anxiety, no fear, no competing, no

2   A. W. Tozer, *Knowledge of the Holy*, reprint edition
    (Los Angeles: Indo-European Publishing, 2018), p. 1.

complaining, no gossiping, judging, or division in the Church. What an extraordinarily attractive bunch of people we would be, having the ability to love one another in preference to ourselves, because of our collective confidence and hope based only on the nature of God! It reminds me of John 13:35 'By this everyone will know that you are my disciples, if you love one another'!

I wonder what picture of God you have in your mind right now. Is He, for example, a bit of an old man with a white beard up in the sky somewhere – a nice ol' guy, but pretty ineffective when it comes to what's going on down here? On the other hand, perhaps He is a strict and harsh headteacher type of character, with a little stick, waiting for you to trip up? Maybe the image is more of an amazing, truly awesome and incredible Creator, but oh so very busy running the universe with no time for your concerns. Or is He some sort of a control freak ruining all your fun, insisting that you live according to His rules? Alternatively, He could be for you an intellectual concept, or even a mixture of all the above, depending on the situations that you find yourself in.

If you see Him like this, *how can you possibly trust Him* with your health, your finances, loved ones, dreams, failures, your shame and your joy? Of course, you can't, and indeed would not want to!

So... *who is he?* How can we have a relationship with Him to the extent that we trust Him 100%? That means 100% of the time, with 100% of who we were, are and will be, thus leaving no room for fear, anxiety or feelings of unworthiness.

God is relational. But what sort of relationship are we talking about? Could it be that of boss and employee, master and servant, teacher and student, or doctor and patient? The Bible tells us from Genesis to Revelation that the way God wants us humans, His beloved created beings, to relate to Him is as *Father*, not as Creator, or Almighty God, or as Saviour of the world. He is, of course, all these, but they are concepts far too big for us to get our finite minds around on a day-to-day basis. Nor are we to relate to Him as doctor, teacher, boss, master – these relationships are far too small, and limited.

In the Old Testament, in Jeremiah 3:19, God says of His children, Israel, 'I thought you would call me "Father" and not turn away', and in Isaiah 63:16 we read, 'But you are our Father, though Abraham does not know us or Israel acknowledge us; you, LORD, are our Father, our Redeemer from of old is your name.' In the New Testament, Jesus Himself says, 'Go … to my brothers and tell them, "I am ascending to my Father and your Father, to my God and your God"' (John 20:17). God's desire is that we relate to Him as a *Father*.

God has never stopped speaking about His longing that we should call Him Father. Of course, it's not just about using the word 'Father', but rather, that the word Father would denote a heart attitude. In ancient Israel, the name you bore was terribly important. A name given at birth was a prophetic pronouncement of who you would become. So, in asking us to call Him Father, God is giving us an invitation into a parent/child relationship. Not because we deserve it, have worked hard for it – not because of our beauty or talents, or spirituality. No. But because of love.

He gives you the choice – so what will *you* call Him?

We know all this in our heads, of course, but do we live every day, when it's tough, when we want to give up, *then*, do we live as sons and daughters, *fully* dependent on our Heavenly Father?

When we went to Pakistan as medical missionaries, our children were still very little. Steve was a general surgeon in those days, and I was a nurse. Serving God in this way had been our dream for many years, both as individuals before we met, but also as a couple. We had spent years planning and preparing. We had gone to Bible college and had travelled the length and breadth of the UK raising financial support. We had endured medicals and psychological tests, language-learning courses, and finally, tearful goodbyes and fierce hugs. You could say we had sacrificed a lot – family, culture, home, friendships, church. For the first few years we struggled with the language barrier, isolation, adapting to new cultural rules and unspoken ways. I, stuck in the house with two small children, was particularly vulnerable. I now see how naive and unrealistic I was in assuming I would effortlessly make local friends, and transition easily from my own culture to this alien and foreign land!

As the 'honeymoon' period wore off, I and my little ones faced many hours alone. Coping with the intense heat, with the fine dust that made its way into every drawer and cupboard, suffering the unconcealed stares of strangers on the street and unable to make myself understood in the marketplace, I began to feel as though God was absent.

God seemed so far away. After all I had given up for Him, I now felt as though I was hitting a brick wall when I prayed or tried to connect with Him, and I could not make sense of it. I felt betrayed and overlooked, as though in some way I had disappointed or displeased God and was now bearing the consequences of this. It didn't take too long before I sank into a pit. Because it felt like He had gone, I concluded that He indeed had, and in so doing, decided that He didn't care and wasn't interested in me. From there, it didn't take too long before I felt unworthy and not up to the task, especially when comparing myself to other 'successful' and seasoned missionaries who surrounded me.

Now, all these years later, I look back and I can see so clearly that for the 10 years that followed, the years dominated by clinical depression, the thoughts in my head that I had about God and what He was like, about me and what He thought of me, were all untrue. I look at the journals that I wrote during those dark days, and see that so often, with large and angry handwriting, each letter was penned with deep pain and much confusion, but the words were not true.

At some point we must decide on our attitude to the Bible.

Does God speak the truth, or not? I don't believe that we can have a pick-and-mix relationship with Scripture, choosing some verses over others, according to our mood or circumstances. When God says He is love, is He or is He not? When He says He forgives us all our sins, does He or does He not? When He says He will never leave us, does He mean it? When He says He heals the broken-hearted, is He teasing? When He says He has good plans for us, to give us hope and a future, is He making that up?

Phoebe, our youngest daughter, spent the first 21 months of her life in an orphanage in Southern China. She knew nothing about us – she did not know that, before her birth, we had started our journey, that we had begun making our way towards her. She did nothing to make that happen. Her adoption was not her reward for good behaviour. Phoebe did not know about her destiny, God's 'red thread' – she had no idea that she was being pursued. It did not cross her mind that she had been chosen, that a plan for her life was unfolding. She just did what babies do. She wasn't even waiting; she was just being.

And do you not think it is the same with us? [3]Abba Father knew us and saw us before the foundation of the world. Down all the years and across the span of time, He calls us – for you see, we think it is we who find Him, but oh no… it is He who finds us.

---

3   The word Abba, found in the bible, is the familiar term for father in many Semitic languages. In English we would say Daddy or Papa.

So, there it is – the red thread that connects us to our Creator, to the one who knows us and who sees us, who has always known and seen us. Our destiny is to be embraced by Father God as His child. We cannot be complete until we find our home in Him – to live as sons and daughters under the protection and provision of the best daddy that there ever was.

As a baby, Phoebe did not know that there was a family who wanted her, who yearned for her to be a part of them – a family who had gone to great lengths, who had waited three years to see their dream come true.

Had she been a little older, she might have doubted that there could be such a family – thousands of miles away, waiting and longing for her to join them? A family from another nation and culture and language, whose ways would be so different from what she was familiar with. She might have said, 'I don't believe that there is anything more to life than this orphanage.' She might have concluded that she was not destined to be lavishly loved, that she would always have to take care of her own needs. That she would always be alone. That she could trust no one. After all, who truly cared about her? Her abandonment as a newborn baby would inevitably dictate her future. How could there be something more? Something better? Something beyond her wildest dreams?

Phoebe would have been wrong. Very wrong. But we are not so very different. We often cannot believe that God has a good plan for us, that He loves us and longs for us. That He has made sacrifices for us. That His desire for us is that we might live abundant lives of joy and peace.

Some of the images we have of God are based on the experiences we have had of our own dads. Some will have been formed by the circumstances of our lives, which have led us to conclude that God is like the old man in the sky or the harsh headteacher, as I explained earlier. There will be several of us whose biological fathers were abusive or neglectful, absent or weak – we were not protected and provided for and made to feel safe. We were not loved and honoured and given dignity and respect by our earthly dads.

I had a great dad. He was a very good man, loving and kind, supportive and caring – but he was not perfect. No human father is perfect, but if I asked you to make a list of the qualities that you would want to see in your dad, I absolutely guarantee that certain characteristics would crop up on your list. They would be on *all* our lists. Surely, we would want a kind father, a loving father, able to accept us as we are. A father who would enjoy our company, who would meet our needs for shelter, food, clothing. A father who was able to give us a sense of security, and who was there for us to run to in times of need. A dad who believed in us. Isn't that the kind of dad we would want?

PAUSE FOR REFLECTION

There will be an opportunity, at the end of each chapter, to reflect a little on what you have just read. So, if you're up for it, grab a notebook and jot down your honest responses to these questions. The first step to freedom is recognising what we *really* believe about God.

1. According to the author Francis Frangipane, 'unless you have glistening hope in every area of your life, you are believing a lie'. Would you say that you have glistening hope in every area of your life? If not, why is that?

2. Describe in three words the character of God as you believe Him to be. Be honest with yourself.

3. Which of the following statements is true for you?

    a. *God is distant and uninterested in me.*
    b. *God does not really care about me.*
    c. *God is absent or too busy to bother with me.*
    d. *God is impatient or angry with me.*
    e. *God no longer forgives me.*
    f. *God does not really love me.*
    g. *God rejects me when I fail to live a sinless life.*

Identifying the lies is a huge step towards freedom! Later, we will look at dismantling them.

4. Do you relate to God as your Abba Daddy?

2

AND, WHAT IS GOD REALLY LIKE?

I sought to hear the voice of God and climbed the topmost steeple,
but God declared: 'Go down again – I dwell among the people.'
JOHN HENRY NEWMAN

So now we come to the crux of the matter – what is this Father God, really like, the One who gives us the right to become part of His family and desires that we should call him Father? How can we be sure, especially if our earthly role-model of a father was not a good one?

In the New Testament, Jesus says of Himself, 'I and the Father are one' (John 10:30). In other words, 'Look at me and then you will know what Father God is really like. We are one and the same. Identical.' The writer of the letter to the Hebrews also describes Him as 'the exact representation' of the Father (Hebrews 1:3). The disciple Philip once said to Jesus, 'Just show us the Father', and Jesus replied something along these lines, and I paraphrase: 'Really? I've been with you all this time? You don't get it, do you? One of the reasons I'm here is so that you can see God in the flesh. If you've seen me, you've seen the Father' (see John 14:9).

In the previous chapter we made a mental note of the fatherly attributes that we would most want to see in our dad. Could we apply these to Jesus? Kind, good, accepting, providing, protecting, someone to turn to in a time of need. Yes, we could. 'If you have seen me, you have seen the Father,' Jesus said.

I can't imagine that there are many people, anywhere on this earth, who would describe Jesus as cruel, or distant, stern and demanding. Do you think Jesus is impatient with you, or angry, controlling or insensitive to your needs? Granted, some say He was only a teacher, a prophet, a good man. Others, that He never existed. But I have never heard anyone say that Jesus is condemning or hard-hearted, unkind or a killjoy. So, I wonder why we think these very same thoughts about our Heavenly Father, when, as we have seen, Jesus and the Father are one. Of course, we wouldn't dare say such a thing out loud, but the thoughts are there somewhere in the back of our minds, prohibiting us from living freely as sons and daughters.

Let me remind you, again. Jesus Himself says that He and the Father are one and that He only did what He saw the Father doing: healing the sick, loving the outcast, forgiving the sinner, honouring women, touching the leper, setting the captives free from emotional and spiritual bondage, feeding the poor, bringing peace in a storm, standing up to injustice and corruption and oppression. He laughs and weeps and eats and drinks and spends time with people. He listens and cares deeply. He understands people's situations and He changes their lives.

This too, then, is *God, the Father*. 'If you have seen me, you have seen the Father.' 'I and the Father are one.'

You will probably know the story of the little girl who is drawing at the kitchen table. When she has finished, she confidently asks, 'Mummy, Mummy, do you want to see what God looks like?' Her mum turns around, surprised, and says, 'Sweetheart, no one knows what God looks like.' But the little girl answers triumphantly, waving her drawing in the air, 'Well, they do now!'

We may not know what God looks like, but we can know what His character is like by 'looking at' Jesus.

It was the 1992 Olympic Games and Derek Redmond was all set to win the gold medal in the 400-metre race. As it began, he surged into the lead, his long athletic legs pounding the track, the finish line, no doubt, already in his mind's eye. But as the track gently veered to the right, Derek, confidently running at a steady pace, suddenly experienced the explosion of a sharp and deep pain in his right leg – his hamstring had snapped. As he seized the injured part, he slowed to a halt and stood in the middle of the track, a thousand thoughts and emotions swirling around in his head, all enveloped in a cloud of searing, relentless and throbbing pain.

'I must do this,' he muttered to himself through clenched teeth, as he painfully hobbled a little further down the track, now a lone figure with thousands of pairs of eyes watching his every move. Then a small commotion occurred behind him, as a man pushed past the security guards and ran onto the track towards the athlete. With tears coursing down his cheeks, Derek now felt the warmth of an arm around his shoulder, a hand gently patting him, and a kind and very familiar voice urging him to stop. His dad. His father.

'You don't have to do this,' his father said, to which Derek replied, 'Oh yes I do.'

'In that case,' replied Jim Redmond, 'we are going to do it together', and leaning on his father's shoulder for support, Derek hobbled the remainder of the lap and completed the race, as the crowd of 65,000 spectators stood to give him a standing ovation.

Watching the YouTube clip of this event conveys to me a powerful message and I am deeply moved – moved because I am witnessing the love of a father for his son and moved because if that is the action of an imperfect, fallen human being, how very huge and wide and deep must be the love of my perfect Heavenly Father. We don't know Jim Redmond but seeing the gesture of compassion and support for his son, we have an idea of what kind of a dad he is. Likewise, we can *watch* Jesus in the Gospels, in the New Testament, and 'see' what kind of father He is revealing to us.

In 'watching' Jesus, in walking with Him through the Gospels, and in seeing how He related to very ordinary people with commonplace problems, we also can observe how the men and women in His world responded to Him. This is really very important for us to understand. We too are invited into a similar relationship with God, because as I have said, in Jesus we have God in the flesh, God incarnate. This is such good news! If Jesus did not react to first-century common, everyday people with criticism, impatience or harsh words, then we need not imagine that that is how God responds to us. If Jesus did not reject or ignore or pass over poor, broken, desperate individuals, then neither will God treat us in that way. Good news indeed! Remember, if you've seen Jesus, you've seen the Father!

With this point in mind, I would like to take you back in time, back to first-century Israel. I am intrigued by a scene in the Gospel of Luke, because this vignette opens a door onto a special friendship between three siblings and Jesus. As I read and think about this incident, my eyes are opened to new opportunities for increased intimacy in my own relationship with God.

If you've never really met Martha, allow me to make the intro-duction. Martha, with her sister Mary and brother Lazarus, lived about 2,000 years ago, in the small Judean town of Bethany, a few miles from Jerusalem. When Jesus was in the area, He would often stop and pay the trio a visit. They would ask Him to stay the night, and if He had to keep moving on, at least He and His disciples would have a meal. It was a wonderful arrangement.

In John 11:1–7, we read that Lazarus – Martha and Mary's brother – has become ill, and subsequently dies.

Now a man named Lazarus was ill. He was from Bethany, the village of Mary and her sister Martha. (This Mary, whose brother Lazarus now lay ill, was the same one who poured perfume on the Lord and wiped his feet with her hair.) So, the sisters sent word to Jesus, 'Lord, the one you love is ill.'

When he heard this, Jesus said, 'This illness will not end in death. No, it is for God's glory so that God's Son may be glorified through it.' Now Jesus loved Martha and her sister and Lazarus. So when he heard that Lazarus was ill, he stayed where he was two more days, and then he said to his disciples, 'Let us go back to Judea.'

These past couple of years we have found ourselves in an extraordinary season – our lives, all our lives, affected in one way or another by Covid 19. The disruption to our routines and rhythms has been huge and, for some of us, nothing will ever be the same again. Martha, too, unexpectedly found herself in a tragic situation, her life turned upside down from one moment to the next.

On his arrival, Jesus found that Lazarus had already been in the tomb for four days. Now Bethany was less than two miles from Jerusalem, and many Jews had come to Martha and Mary to comfort them in the loss of their brother. When Martha heard that Jesus was coming, she went out to meet him, but Mary stayed at home.

'Lord,' Martha said to Jesus, 'if you had been here, my brother would not have died. But I know that even now God will give you whatever you ask.'

(John 11:17–22)

In verse 21 Martha says to Jesus, 'Lord, if you had been here, my brother would not have died.' A 'no holding back' response. Perhaps, by reading in-between the lines, we can sense that what she was saying was something more like, 'Where have you been? You are the only one who can help us. We are your friends, and you should have come when we needed you. He's dead because you weren't here to heal him.' Nonetheless, what we do know is that, in speaking as she did, she poured out her complaint to Jesus with brutal honesty.

I believe Martha is deeply disappointed in Jesus, perhaps even feeling a sense of betrayal. These three siblings were Jesus' very dear friends; their home was His home – a place for Him to rest and take refuge from the demanding crowds that followed Him everywhere. I think they would have known each other very well. Over a three-year period, without doubt, they had enjoyed meals together, laughter and challenging conversations.

Just imagine the emotions and thoughts swirling around Martha's head when Jesus chose *not* to come immediately to Bethany – when He chose to stay on an extra couple of days. Two women would now be left with no male protection, leaving them, in that culture, vulnerable and exposed. There was no National Health Service, no medications or clever doctors. With Lazarus this ill, their only hope was Jesus. We can presume that Martha had heard about all the wonderful and miraculous healings that Jesus had been doing. She knew that He loved them, and yet... Lazarus had died with no *apparent* effort on Jesus' behalf to turn this awful situation around, or even just to be there with them. I think she would have been very, very disappointed. She knew that He could have arrived earlier, had He wanted to. She exposes the rawness of her heart in that 'no holding back' statement that she makes: 'If you had been here, my brother would not have died.' Martha might well have been thinking, *well, maybe He doesn't really want to be with us. Perhaps He doesn't care as much as I thought He did. Actually, He's probably too busy – what's one more illness to Him when so many are in need?* Do we not think along similar lines, when it seems to us that God has not heard the cry of our heart?

Many of us step away from God in our pain and grief as though we can't quite bear the presence of the only One who *can* answer our longings but seems not to want to. Or so we believe.

Earlier, on another occasion, this time recorded in Luke (10:40), Martha is in the middle of making sandwiches that Jesus had probably not actually ordered, and frustration and irritation is building up inside her at not being assisted by Mary. Suddenly Martha blurts out to Jesus, 'Don't you care that my sister has left me to do the work by myself? Tell her to help me!' Again, another 'no holding back' response. She did not pretend that she was happy with this arrangement. She did not withdraw, to sulk in the kitchen. She did not suppress her feelings out of politeness or out of wanting to look super-spiritual or even in order to impress Jesus.

When was the last time you poured out your complaint, your frustration, your anger in total honesty to God? Revealing our deepest needs takes nothing away from His love for us, but rather is an indication of our very real trust in Him. When we know that we are loved by God, there is space there for the whole of who we are, not just the nice, kind parts but also the selfish, irritated, annoyed parts too. The love of God is so vast that it can shoulder the whole of who we really are – the broken alongside the healed, the pain and the joy, the hope and the hopelessness.

Covid-19 surely exposed, in us all, the best, the good, the bad and the downright ugly in human nature. Perhaps real fear surfaced at that time and continues to do so. Or a deep sense of anxiety began to reveal itself. Even outrage at the unfairness of life in those months – some seemed to sail through while we struggled emotionally, financially and relationally. The pandemic apart, life itself will undoubtedly throw stuff at us that is unexpected or shocking or confusing – we are confronted with evil, with injustice, with deep loss and with unanswered prayer. How we process these traumas is important. I think we often tend to just mutter and murmur to ourselves, or to others. We complain and grumble, or sometimes we boil and rage, as if He who sees everything cannot see our distress. We often choose to present ourselves to God in a certain 'acceptable' way. We don't want Him to see the bits of us that we don't like. We somehow think that in seeing the 'real' me, He would have to turn away, or His love for us might grow cold.

We cannot *really* know God as a close, loving and wonderful father unless we are willing to be vulnerable. Only when our deepest self is exposed to Him, and only when we stop covering up our pain, only then can true love be cultivated. Only then can we really experience joy, as Martha did later, at the raising of her brother.

Martha knew this. Her response to Jesus is a fine example for us of how to deal with our confusion and doubts. Our God is not distant or cruel; He is not demanding or critical; He is not uninterested or uncaring. He can shoulder it all!

And Jesus Himself does indeed beckon to us in our weariness and in our bewilderment when he says:

> Come to me, all you who are weary and burdened, and I will give you rest. Take my yoke upon you and learn from me, for I am gentle and humble in heart, and you will find rest for your souls. For my yoke is easy and my burden is light.
>
> (Matthew 11:28–30)

We have glanced briefly at Jesus' interaction with Martha at a difficult time, giving us an example of how we might also approach Him with raw honesty. I want us to also have a look at how Jesus related to His Heavenly Father. Their relationship can act as a guide to our relationship with God as our Father. It teaches us how we can talk to Him. We learn from Jesus the kind of interaction that it is possible for us to also have with our Heavenly Father, for He is our brother, as He acknowledges in Mark 3:34 (ESV): 'And looking about at those who sat around him, he said, "Here are my mother and my brothers!"'

I think the most powerful example that the New Testament gives us of how Jesus related to God the Father is found in the Garden of Gethsemane. Here we are invited into a profoundly intimate and vulnerable moment in the life of Jesus. He knows that His time on earth is up. He knows that crucifixion lies ahead. His heart is breaking at what He must endure and at the price that He will have to pay:

> Going a little farther, he fell to the ground and prayed that if possible the hour might pass from him. '*Abba*, Father,' he said, 'everything is possible for you. Take this cup from me. Yet not what I will, but what you will.'
>
> (Mark 14:35–36)

There is no pretence here. No withdrawing from what He must face. No hiding the inner turmoil He is experiencing. We see real deep emotion expressed by Jesus to His Abba, His daddy.

Again, as with Martha, we are confronted with a God who is not remote, cold or uninterested after all, or waiting for us to trip up. In Jesus' moment of raw vulnerability, He knows that He will be heard by His Father.

Paul, in Galatians 4:6, reminds us that Jesus' Abba is also *our* Abba, our daddy, too: 'Because you are his sons [by inference, and daughters], God sent the Spirit of his Son into our hearts, the Spirit who calls out, "*Abba*, Father"', and in Romans 8:16 (ESV): 'you have received the Spirit of adoption as sons [and daughters], by whom we cry, "Abba! Father!"' Even way back in the time of Isaiah, the prophet named the coming Messiah as Father: 'For unto us a child is born, unto us a son is given: and the government shall be upon his shoulder: and his name shall be called Wonderful, Counsellor, The mighty God, The everlasting Father, The Prince of Peace' (Isaiah 9:6 KJV). This baby would be the means by which all of humankind would be given the opportunity to know the Creator of the world, intimately, as Father.

Crouching in that corner in our house in Gilgit, in the mountains of Northern Pakistan, all those many years ago, I felt hopeless. I have had to walk a long road for me to sort myself out. On our premature return from Gilgit, I knew that I could not provide the answer to the inner yearnings and longings for authentic connection with God that I so desperately longed for. I read the New Testament writer's words of freedom and faith and childlike trust but did not seem to be able to drum up enough of anything to bring lasting change. I felt truly stuck.

On the quest to live a life that, at least in part, reflected some of the truths that I read about in my daily devotional times, I stumbled upon this profound revelation: I realised that I knew a lot about God in my head – I had been to Bible college, after all – but this knowledge had somehow never made the journey to my heart. I did not really know God.

If we do not have a genuinely honest and uniquely personal relationship with the only One in the universe who has always seen us and known us, it is more than likely that trusting Him will be problematic for us. And it's because we cannot fully trust God's ability to parent us well, to provide for us, to protect us, to take care of the precious people in our lives, that we are insecure and unsure, anxious and fearful.

At some point, I believe, we have to make a choice. If in Jesus we are seeing the Father in action, then in the Holy Spirit we also encounter His nature – love, and joy, peace, patience and goodness, faithfulness, kindness, gentleness and self-control. This is the Father. This is the Trinity; the character of the Godhead is reflected in each member of the Trinity. God has not left us in the dark – He has displayed His character openly for all to see. There can be no doubt about what He is really like.

The choice that lies before us is this. Will we choose to take Him at His word, or will we decide to put our feelings, the circumstances of our lives, and the narrative that our culture is speaking, over and above the words that God speaks?

God, in creating us, knows that we need a dad – all of us. Even those of us who are older still need a dad. In Himself, He has provided us with the best father that there has ever been. No matter how we feel, no matter what happens to us, He is our dad – and we are His sons and daughters. The Bible says that God is love (1 John 4:8). He can only be the best dad ever. Love defines Him, love motivates Him, love fuels Him, love drives Him. He is love.

In the twenty-first century, the world needs a dad more than ever before in the history of humankind. We now know that children from fatherless homes are more likely to be poor, drop out of school, and suffer from health and emotional problems. Boys with absent dads are more likely to become involved in crime, and girls without the loving influence of a father are more likely to become pregnant as teens.

The US Department of Health and Human Services states, 'Fatherless children are at a dramatically greater risk of drug and alcohol abuse.'[4] Here are some other alarming statistics:

> Children in father-absent homes are almost four times more likely to be poor. In 2011, 12% of children in married-couple families were living in poverty, compared to 44 percent of children in mother-only families.[5]

---

4   US Department of Health and Human Services, National Center for Health Statistics, *Survey on Child Health* (Washington, DC: 1993).

5   US Census Bureau, *Children's Living Arrangements and Characteristics: March 2011* (Washington, DC: 2011), Table C8.

Children aged 10 to 17 living with two biological or adoptive parents were significantly less likely to experience sexual assault, child maltreatment, other types of major violence, and non-victimization type of adversity, and were less likely to witness violence in their families compared to peers living in single-parent families and stepfamilies.[6]

According to 72.2 % of the U.S. population, fatherlessness is the most significant family or social problem facing America.[7]

The American website www.fathers.com states that more than 20 million children live in a home without the physical presence of a father. Millions more have dads who are physically present, but emotionally absent. If it were classified as a disease, fatherlessness would be an epidemic worthy of attention as a national emergency. The impact of fatherlessness can be seen in homes, schools, hospitals and prisons. In short, the website states that fatherlessness is associated with almost every societal ill facing American children. And we all know that the issue is not just an American one.

With this very worrying situation in mind, it is my passionate belief that if we, the Church, if we, God's beloved children, could live every day in relationship with God as our Heavenly Abba Father, then our families and communities, our towns

---

6   Heather A. Turner, 'The Effect of Lifetime Victimization on the Mental Health of Children and Adolescents', *Social Science & Medicine*, Vol. 62, No. 1 (January 2006), pp. 13–27.
7   National Center for Fathering, 'Fathering in America' Poll, January 1999.

and cities, and even our nations, could look very different from how they do currently. The world is crying out for fathers, and we have the extraordinary privilege of knowing the one true and perfect Father of all fathers. This father is the only one who accepts us as we are; He is the only one who won't let us down; He won't abandon us, reject us, or die; He won't betray us or humiliate us. This is *the* father that we can introduce to our needy and troubled world, but if we don't know Him ourselves, if we only know *about* Him with head knowledge, if our relationships are fuelled by stress and tension, then the invitation that we extend, and the testimony of our lives are not actually particularly attractive.

Right now, there is no greater task that you can set yourself than the goal of getting to really know your Heavenly Father. This is more important than anything else – more important than what you do *for* Him. When you know that you know that you know that He is good, that He will *never* let you down, never leave you, that you are His adored child, *then* you are surely the happiest of people, and your joy will be complete.

The main point that I would love you to take away with you from these first two chapters is this: I have said that in Jesus we see the Father's character, His nature, and what He is truly like. Could you take a moment to consider that the image of God that you carry in your head may not be accurate, even though you may sincerely believe it to be true? If what we believe about God is anything other than Biblical truth, then we will not be able to trust Him completely and utterly, in all situations. We may need, therefore, to rethink and re-evaluate.

Recognising our own misunderstanding in relation to what God is really like is the first big step towards freedom. If we are willing to admit that we may be believing a lie or an inaccuracy about who God actually is, we are already moving in the right direction towards freedom from anxiety, fear and insecurity. If we choose to do nothing about righting our incorrect understanding of who God is, we will never be truly free. From personal experience, and from years of mentoring young women and from hours of one-to-one deeper prayer ministry, I have witnessed a very real struggle in many. However, by making the bold and courageous decision to believe what God says about Himself, we place ourselves on the path to healing and wholeness. It is not a quick fix, it takes guts and tenacity, and it may take a while, but surely, it's what we all want: '*It is for freedom* that Christ has set us free' (Galatians 5:1, italics mine).

For me, the understanding and realisation that I can truly trust the nature of God, as a loving Father, has come gradually and quietly over several years as I have chosen to believe that He is who He says He is. I do not want my life and faith to be dictated by my feelings or to be defined by past experiences. He says that I am His beloved child, that He sees me and knows me, that I am His dwelling place and that He values me. Choosing to believe these truths has transformed my life. Today, I rest in Him. I now live most days with a deep sense of peace and contentment.

I now choose to believe God. I choose to relate to Him as the best dad ever, the sort of father that has the characteristics that we listed earlier. I choose to rest in the revelation that He is my Father, my Abba Daddy, that He is always for me and not against me; that He has good plans for me, no matter what happens; and that He is always kind and gentle towards me (Romans 8:31; Jeremiah 29:11; 31:3). I'm not perfect at it, but I am intentional about it. Of course, I have down days and difficult days – I struggle and sometimes I kick and scream – but in general, I live with a deep sense of peace as I continually choose truth, even when it is hard, really hard to do so. Bit by bit, the theology of God as my Father is becoming a heartfelt reality, and *it can be yours*. Let Him father you well, as only He can do. The love of the Father makes us complete – it is all we have ever needed.

PAUSE FOR REFLECTION

1. Believing lies about the character of God can contribute greatly to anxiety, fear and depression. Can you see how this might be true for you?

2. By 'watching' how Jesus lived and behaved, we are shown what the Father is like. Jesus Himself says, in John 10:30, 'I and the Father are one.' Is this a new thought for you? How does it make you feel?

3. Having discovered that Jesus reveals the nature of the Father to us, can you now see that God might not be who you think He is? Would you be prepared to acknowledge that what you think about God's character as Father may be inaccurate, or even a lie, although it may *feel* very true?

3

WHO IS THE DEVIL?

There is no neutral ground in the universe. Every square inch, every split second, is claimed by God, and counterclaimed by Satan.
C. S. LEWIS

Although the devil appears in various forms in many of the world's religions and can be compared to some mythological gods, as Christians, we know the devil to be the adversary of God and of God's people.

The devil is present throughout the Bible. From the beginning to the end, he is there, though sometimes not as obviously as at other times. We don't want to go overboard and see demons everywhere and in everything, but nor can we afford to ignore him. Our scientific humanistic culture, of course, does not acknowledge the devil, but then so many do not acknowledge God either. We need to be balanced, and we must be informed and aware; otherwise, we will be caught off guard when we least expect it.

The devil first shows up in the book of Genesis as the serpent who convinced Eve – who then persuaded Adam – to eat the forbidden fruit from the 'tree of the knowledge of good and evil' in the Garden of Eden. After Eve fell for the devil's conniving ways, she and Adam were banished from the Garden, forever. This is our first introduction to the devil.

It is crucial then that we, as followers of Jesus, understand who the devil is and what his role is likely to be in our lives. If Jesus had confrontations with the devil, then we most surely will. It is a surprise to me how few believers truly understand how this enemy of ours attacks us, and therefore, how to respond to his tactics.

Paul, the apostle, says this in Ephesians 6:11: 'Put on the full armour of God, so that you can take your stand against the devil's schemes.' Clearly, the devil has schemes. He will most definitely direct his attention towards us, but we have also been provided with spiritual armour in order to protect and defend ourselves.

Unless we are fully aware of the devil's plans, we will never be free of the things that hold us back, that keep us locked into anxiety and fear. Until we understand the devil's schemes, we will never be free of the insecurities and jealousies and struggles that so often spoil our relationships, add stress to our lives, and stop us from moving forward, in freedom.

Graham A. Cole has written extensively about the devil and

demons. Here he discusses a 'blind spot' that many of us suffer from:

> Paul G. Hiebert was raised in India but trained in the West as an anthropologist and sociologist. He came to realise that his western training had made him become unaware of the activity of spirits both good and evil, which most of the world has never actually lost sight of. He called this blind spot 'the flaw of the excluded middle.' He thought that many western Christians may have an espoused theology affirming angels and demons, but in practice have an operational theology that lives as though God and ourselves were the only intelligences.[8]

This western Christian view does not serve us well, in that many of us live our days totally unaware of the many schemes and tactics used by the devil to rob us of all that Christ died to give us – joy and hope and love and peace, and so so much more! Jesus, himself says this, reminding us that, 'the thief comes only to steal and kill and destroy. I came that they may have life and have it abundantly.'

To start with, I want to get a few facts straight about the devil. In the Bible he is referred to by other names and descriptions, including Satan, the enemy, Lucifer, the serpent, the dragon, the prince of darkness, Beelzebub, the antichrist, murderer ... and I could go on. We don't know a huge amount about his origins, but we don't need to! What we do need to know and

---

8   Graham Cole Crossway.org/articles/10 things you should know about Demons and Satan

remember, however, is that the Bible explicitly teaches that the devil was totally and utterly defeated at the cross and that Jesus is the victor!

It seems that the devil was created as an angelic being, but set himself up against God, in pride, and was subsequently rejected from Heaven:

> How you have fallen from heaven,
>   morning star, son of the dawn!
> You have been cast down to the earth,
>   you who once laid low the nations!
> You said in your heart,
>   'I will ascend to the heavens;
> I will raise my throne
>   above the stars of God;
> I will sit enthroned on the mount of assembly,
>   on the utmost heights of Mount Zaphon.
> I will ascend above the tops of the clouds;
>   I will make myself like the Most High.'
> But you are brought down to the realm of the dead,
>   To the depths of the pit.

> (Isaiah 14:12–15)

The devil is a spirit, and he can assume different forms. We have already encountered him as a snake in the Garden of Eden, but the New Testament also says this about him: 'Satan himself masquerades as an angel of light' (2 Corinthians 11:14).

He has an army of lesser malevolent spiritual beings, demons, who do his bidding, as we are reminded in Ephesians 6:12: 'For our struggle is not against flesh and blood, but against the rulers, against the authorities, against the powers of this dark world and against the spiritual forces of evil in the heavenly realms.'

It is really important to understand that the devil is not like God in any shape or form. He is not omnipresent – he himself cannot be in more than one location at any one time, although of course he has demons carrying out his orders all over the place. Neither is this enemy omniscient – he does not know everything, although he can clearly influence our thinking, and put thoughts in our minds.

I believe that Judas's heart was already inclined towards evil, and the devil took advantage of that. We are told in John 13:2 that, 'The evening meal was in progress, and the devil had already prompted Judas, the son of Simon Iscariot, to betray Jesus.' Likewise, Ananias in Acts chapter 5 unashamedly lied to Peter about his wealth, and the deceit is attributed to the influence of Satan: 'Then Peter said, "Ananias, how is it that Satan has so filled your heart that you have lied to the Holy Spirit and have kept for yourself some of the money you received for the land?"' (Acts 5:3). In the Old Testament, Satan is credited with encouraging David to organise a census of Israel, so that he might know how many fighting men there were: 'Satan rose up against Israel and incited David to take a census of Israel' (1 Chronicles 21:1). The dictionary defines the word 'incite' as 'to motivate, to prompt or to provoke'. King David was tempted to take his eyes off God as his protector and to place his faith on the number of men who were in his army, thus trusting instead in his own resources.

These three examples demonstrate how the enemy might prompt, provoke or motivate us to think in a particular way. Had Judas, Ananias or King David recognised that these thoughts were demonic in origin, surely none of them would have entertained them, let alone acted upon them. In fact, Judas, on realising where his actions had led, hanged himself. All three examples ended in catastrophe for those involved.

The Screwtape Letters, written by C. S. Lewis, is a great little book that helpfully describes the possible ways in which demons interact with us daily. We are not possessed by them, remember, but we can, as we have seen from the above Biblical examples, be significantly influenced by them. The book records a series of letters written by a senior demon, Screwtape, to a lesser, junior one, named Wormwood. The latter is being mentored in the ways of incitement and deceit in his interactions with a particular young man who is an atheist but being drawn to Jesus.

At one point in the story, Screwtape tells Wormwood about a 'patient' he once had who was an atheist (meaning a human he was assigned to), who, like the young man, was also an atheist. One day this man was reading in the British Museum and began to think 'the wrong way', according to the demon – that is, he started to think that God might exist after all. Instantly,

God quietly encouraged the atheist to pursue this new line of thought. The demon's only defence, then, was to distract the 'patient' with thoughts of food, and the need to have lunch, suggesting to him that it would be much better to 'come back after lunch and go into it with a fresh mind'. During the man's break away from the museum, Screwtape further diverted him with the hustle and bustle of 'real life' until the patient had safely decided that his earlier train of thought, while 'shut up alone with his books', just couldn't possibly be true![9]

In C. S. Lewis's attempt to impress upon his readers how the devil influences our thinking, he beautifully illustrates the ordinariness of his strategies, and how essential it is that we be vigilant and wise to the subtle tactics he so often uses.

The devil can hear our words and will use situations and life events as opportunities to potentially weaken us. Unlike God, the devil is not creative – he uses the same old tactics repeatedly, twisting and spoiling God's good intentions into something ugly and deceitful. Whenever you see a genuine work of the Spirit of God, the devil will always have his imitation. Satan's business specializes in flooding the market with cheap imitations, thus clouding the issues. As a result, people have difficulty discerning between the truth and lies.

This lack of any originality is to our advantage. The strategies the devil used when he lured Eve into eating the fruit in the

9 C. S. Lewis, *The Screwtape Letters: Letters from a Senior to a Junior Devil* (London: William Collins, 2012), pp. 2–3.

garden, so very long ago, are the same strategies he uses today, and we will look at these in more detail in a later chapter.

Let's look at some of the things that the Bible has to say about the devil's character.

Jesus says this about the devil: 'When he lies, he speaks his native language, for he is a liar and the father of lies' (John 8:44). Paul describes him as 'the prince of the power of the air' (Ephesians 2:2 KJV), and John tells us that the devil 'accuses [Christians] day and night' (Revelation 12:10 ESV).

And he is clearly cruel and fierce: 'Be sober-minded; be watchful. Your adversary the devil prowls around like a roaring lion, seeking someone to devour' (1 Peter 5:8 ESV). The image of a bloodthirsty, hungry lion on the prowl, looking for weaker prey to pick off, is indeed a sobering picture.

As I said before, we must keep in mind that the devil was completely defeated at the cross. His power is limited and there is no need to ever be afraid of him. The Bible clearly teaches that God within us is greater, far greater, than the devil who is roaming around out there. But, in the same way that while trekking through the jungle, you would keep an eye out for snakes, but not miss the wonders and beauty that surround you, so we too must live our lives to the full, while also being aware of the enemy's tactics and wily ways.

Paul says this of Jesus: 'When He had disarmed the rulers and authorities [those supernatural forces of evil operating against us], He made a public example of them [exhibiting them as captives in His triumphal procession], having triumphed over them through the cross' (Colossians 2:15 AMP). The reason that the Son of God appeared was to destroy the devil's work, and this He did. On the cross, Jesus cried, 'It is finished' (John 19:30), before giving up His spirit.

The devil hates God. I have heard it said that as he can't get to Him, instead he goes for what is most dear and most precious to God – His treasured sons and daughters. It is my conviction that although he can't affect our status as 'the beloved of God', if he can get us to doubt who we are and to doubt who God is, then he's done a lot of damage. If he can influence you in such a way that you doubt God's goodness and that God loves you lavishly and unconditionally, he has accomplished much. Above all, the devil is a narcissist. He desires that all of humanity worship him, take note of him, follow him, listen to him.

The devil cannot take our salvation away from us. Having put our faith in Jesus, we are firmly planted in the kingdom of God, and Satan cannot remove us. This may come as a surprise to you, but he has no power over us, other than what we give him. Jesus makes this clear in saying to us, 'I have given you authority …. over all the power of the enemy' (Luke 10:19 ESV).

The devil can, however, cause us to lead small and diminished lives, hampered by doubt and fear, and this is because we have not understood the nature of his schemes and the intentions behind them. Neither have we fully grasped the extraordinary position that God's great grace has granted us through the blood of Jesus. We cannot afford to be complacent, or apathetic. It will not benefit us to ignore the power of evil or bury our heads in the sand when it comes to issues regarding the devil and his devious, manipulative and lying ways. We are in a battle. The war has been won and we know the end of the story, but for a season the devil has been allowed, by God, to roam the earth, to be the prince of the power of the air, and he wreaks a lot of havoc and does a lot of damage.

We read in Ephesians 4:27, 'do not give the enemy a foothold'. A foothold can be best understood by imagining yourself being chased by a bad person. You run up to your room and try to close the door, but the person sticks his shoe in at the bottom end of the door so you can't close it. That part of his foot that prevents you from closing the door effectively is called a 'foothold'. A foothold is very dangerous. It gives a thief and other evil people the chance to threaten you, cause you to fret or panic, throw things at you, and ultimately it gives them an opportunity to eventually break in. While the thief has his foot in your door, you are not safe – you cannot continue to live your life in peace. With this particular verse in mind, 'do not give the enemy a foothold', I want to consider, briefly, two major factors that constitute a 'foothold' in spiritual terms.

Firstly, when we refuse to forgive those who have harmed and hurt us, we most definitely create an opportunity for the door of our lives to be pushed open, allowing access to demons.

Unforgiveness is like the shoe wedging the door open – it is an entry point for the devil. Secondly, when we agree with the lies that he whispers to us, and thereby allow them to inform and shape our relationship with God, again we are allowing him to stick his foot into the door of our lives. We will be looking at lies and the subject of forgiveness in more detail in later chapters.

Persistent and unrepentant sin in our lives offers the devil another entry point, as does any activity involving occult practices – horoscopes, Ouija boards, horror films, visiting mediums, tarot cards, to name but a few. These are expressly forbidden in Scripture. God alone knows where we have been and where we are going: '"For I know the plans I have for you," declares the LORD, "plans to prosper you and not to harm you, plans to give you hope and a future"' (Jeremiah 29:11). Messing about with these activities will do us no good even though they may seem to be harmless.

Let me say once again: the devil cannot possess you. As a follower of Jesus, you belong to God and the Holy Spirit indwells you, but Satan can **oppress** you, and cause you to live a less than the abundant life promised by Jesus.

* * *

The opening minutes of the film *Dunkirk* introduce us to a bleak and desolate scene: pieces of paper are falling like snow, fluttering gently down through cold grey skies and onto the derelict, empty streets of an abandoned town – broken wooden shutters, hanging loosely from their hinges, creak in the breeze. We see six young soldiers rummaging in rubbish bins and poking their pale and drawn faces through broken and shattered windowpanes, their bodies tense, alert, nervous. The paper continues to fall, dancing lightly, randomly, until it hits the ground. One soldier crouches down to check a coiled garden hose and tries the tap – nothing. Another plucks a handful of paper from the air and half-heartedly examines the bold, depressing words. Propaganda leaflets have been dropped in their millions for their benefit, potential food for serious thought, penned to induce fear and terror in these young hearts: 'You are surrounded'. He screws up the hideous thing and throws it to the ground deliberately and intentionally.

A little later in the film, we are confronted with another scene: hundreds of boats, both great and small, are putting out to sea on one of the most extraordinary rescue missions recorded. The evacuation of the British Expeditionary Force and other Allied troops from the French seaport of Dunkirk to England, had begun. When it ended on June 4th, 1940, about 198,000 British and 140,000 French and Belgian troops had been saved, and yes, of course, many lives were also lost, but remarkably few, given the odds stacked against them. Unbeknown to those six young soldiers roaming the deserted streets amid a flurry of propaganda, being surrounded by the enemy was only part of the picture – the other part was the imminent rescue of hundreds of thousands of Allied troops.

The enemy of our souls is a huge propaganda merchant. He thrives on deception, intimidation and emotional manipulation, using the circumstances of our lives to feed us the lies he knows we will probably swallow because that is what the current narrative and often our emotions seem to be telling us. But with God, there is always another bigger, redemptive truth to step into!

 PAUSE FOR REFLECTION

1. When you hear the words 'devil', 'Satan', 'the evil one', 'the enemy', what thoughts or images come to mind?

2. Are you aware of the ways in which the devil attacks you? Do you recognise him when he assaults your mind?

3. Jesus says, 'I have given *you* authority ... over all the power of the enemy' (Luke 10:19 ESV, italics mine). Did you know this? Do you live each day confident in your position (see Ephesians 2:6) and authority in Christ?

4

FORGIVE? REALLY?

I have decided to stick with love. Hate is too great a burden to bear.
MARTIN LUTHER KING JR

Over the years, I have read many books and have attended numerous excellent Christian conferences, and in doing so, I have positioned myself at the feet of wonderful saints – brothers and sisters who are running ahead of me in every way. I may not remember now much of what I gleaned then, but in the same way that I don't remember what I ate on Tuesday evening two weeks ago yet know that my body was nourished by the good food, so likewise my spirit was deeply enriched. However, there is some teaching that I will not forget – indeed, must never forget – and yet, if spoken of at all, it is not taught well in our churches. Forgiveness. One simple word, one profound principle, one significant key, perhaps the *most* significant key available to us in our desire to live full and abundant lives, free from fears.

Let's start by reading together a parable spoken by Jesus, and found in Matthew 18:23–35:

> Therefore, the kingdom of heaven is like a king who wanted to settle accounts with his servants. As he began the settlement, a man who owed him ten thousand bags of gold was brought to him. Since he was not able to pay, the master ordered that he and his wife and his children and all that he had be sold to repay the debt.
>
> At this the servant fell on his knees before him. 'Be patient with me,' he begged, 'and I will pay back everything.' The servant's master took pity on him, cancelled the debt and let him go.
>
> But when that servant went out, he found one of his fellow servants who owed him a hundred silver coins. He grabbed him and began to choke him. 'Pay back what you owe me!' he demanded.
>
> His fellow servant fell to his knees and begged him, 'Be patient with me, and I will pay it back.'
>
> But he refused. Instead, he went off and had the man thrown into prison until he could pay the debt. When the other servants saw what had happened, they were outraged and went and told their master everything that had happened.
>
> Then the master called the servant in. 'You wicked servant,' he said, 'I cancelled all that debt of yours because you begged me to. Shouldn't you have had mercy on your fellow servant just as I had on you?' In anger his master handed him over to the jailers to be tortured, until he should pay back all he owed.
>
> This is how my heavenly Father will treat each of you unless you forgive your brother or sister from your heart.

The king, of course, is God, and we are the servants. We have all stood before the great King, owing him 10,000 bags of gold, and more – too much to even count (equal to the income gained over 150,000 years of work for a first-century farmer or peasant!). Not one of us could ever even imagine being able to repay such a sum until, suddenly, there and then, the King Himself, standing before us, cancels the entire debt! Wow! What…? The King extravagantly, abundantly and illogically pays what was rightfully his due.

In failing to forgive those who have hurt us, we are rejecting the gift of forgiveness extended to us by our King. The consequences of not forgiving, or of refusing to forgive, keep us bound and in the darkness of our own bitterness and anger, nursing old hurts and betrayals, never really free to live the generous and wholehearted life God created us to enjoy in all its blessing, bounty and fullness.

Remember again Galatians 5:1: 'It is for freedom that Christ has set us free. Stand firm, then, and do not let yourselves be burdened again by a yoke of slavery.' It seems, then, that we can let ourselves be burdened by a yoke, and thus not experience the freedom that Jesus has given us. In the context of freedom, forgiveness is a big deal. By not forgiving, we will most definitely be submitting ourselves to a yoke of slavery. Let me say it straight: if you don't forgive those who have hurt you, in time you may well become bitter and twisted and limited in your relationship with God. Lack of forgiveness stunts spiritual growth. The yoke you will bear enslaves you in bondage to bitterness.

God is relational and it is His greatest desire that His people are part of a supportive, caring, worldwide community where we have responsibility for each other and where His ways, though they may seem upside down and inside out, nonetheless compel us to generously extend radical and abundant grace to one another, in the sure knowledge that we ourselves are on the receiving end of His extravagant affection and mercy. In addressing the issue of forgiveness, Paul makes this extraordinary counter-intuitive statement: 'If your enemy is hungry, feed him; if he is thirsty, give him something to drink. In doing this, you will heap burning coals on his head' (Romans 12:20).

It doesn't matter who you are, or what you believe. You might be a follower of Jesus, or not. You might be a Muslim, an atheist, a Buddhist. Forgiveness is a principle that God has instituted, and all men and women and children everywhere are affected by not forgiving.

Howard Zehr, an American criminologist and pioneer of the modern concept of 'restorative justice', initially popularised this term, and in the 1990s its use greatly expanded. In the 2000s, the term began to appear in United Nations and European Union documents, illustrating that restorative justice had become an internationally recognised pathway to justice. This approach to crime, as described on the Restorative Justice Council website, brings those harmed by conflict and those responsible for the harm into communication, enabling everyone affected by a particular incident to play a part in repairing the harm and finding a positive way forward.

Writing about forgiveness as applied to the process of restorative justice, and from a non-religious point of view, Ari Kohen, from the Department of Political Science, University of Nebraska–Lincoln, Lincoln, USA, says this: 'forgiveness is not necessarily a religious concept, contrary to common perception … it is through the experience of forgiving offenders that victims are empowered and can gain access to all that a restorative process offers.' He later continues in the same article:

> one of the most powerful aspects of forgiveness is that it allows victims to reassert their power over their own lives. In this sense, the experience of restorative justice – with its emphasis on forgiving, letting go of the offense – offers victims the possibility of both healing and empowerment. In order to gain access to these positive possible outcomes of restorative justice, victims must choose to begin the difficult work of forgiving offenders for the harm they caused …[10]

The parable of the unmerciful servant is a sobering one. So often, we come to God seeking mercy for ourselves, 'Please, please forgive me,' we plead. And yet, towards others who have wronged us and hurt us, we want judgement, crying 'I will never forgive him for what he did!' I'm afraid it doesn't work like that. God shows us mercy, so that we would be merciful to others, releasing them from receiving what they deserve. Likewise, His grace extends to us that which we don't

10 Ari Kohen, 'The Personal and the Political: Forgiveness and Reconciliation in Restorative Justice', *Critical Review of International Social and Political Philosophy*, Vol. 12, No. 3 (2009), pp. 399–423. https://doi.org/10.1080/13698230903127911

deserve! C. S. Lewis famously put it like this, 'To be a Christian means to forgive the inexcusable because God has forgiven the inexcusable in you'.[11]

Jesus speaks these words to us in Matthew 5:43–45: 'You have heard that it was said, "Love your neighbour and hate your enemy." But I tell you, love your enemies and pray for those who persecute you, that you may be children of your Father in heaven. He causes his sun to rise on the evil and the good and sends rain on the righteous and the unrighteous.'

When we do not forgive from our hearts, we are often emotionally and psychologically tormented by what we have suffered, as the parable depicts. As in verse 34 of the passage quoted earlier from Matthew 18, you could say that we are handed over 'to be tortured'. We live with great pain at the thought of the injustice; we flinch at any reminder of that particular person. Some of us will grow bitter and twisted, cynical and unable to trust ever again. There is no doubt about it that if you fail to forgive from your heart, you will suffer consequences, to a lesser or greater extent, around that issue of injury in your life. Paul, again, writing to the Ephesians, encourages us to: 'Get rid of all bitterness, rage and anger, brawling and slander, along with every form of malice. Be kind and compassionate to one another, forgiving each other, just as in Christ God forgave you' (Ephesians 4:31–32). True forgiveness brings peace.

---

11 C. S. Lewis, 'On Forgiveness', in *The Weight of Glory* (New York: HarperCollins, 2001), p. 182.

Let me share with you Sharon's story, told in her own words, and with her kind permission:

I was filled with The Holy Spirit in 1997 and experienced love, peace and security in my life for the very first time. However, there was a huge dark cloud over me due to unforgiveness, hurt and pain ... I had been estranged from my family, and in particular, from my mother, for many years.

The relationship I had with my mother and the things that she'd said and done had crushed the very core of my being and for many years I was locked in a prison of hatred and anger towards her, and I couldn't even say the word mother without breaking out into a strawberry-like rash all over my body. This was literally the buried anger and pain coming to the surface every time her name was mentioned.

My thinking towards her was extremely toxic and the only solace I could find to ease the pain was the hope of someday getting revenge and reciprocating the hurt that she'd caused me.

As a new Christian, I'd given the Lord many areas of my life to redeem, but I'd never given him my mother ... *until* ... one day in December 2000 when everything changed.

I was alone in the house and the telephone rang. It was my aunt who I hadn't spoken to for many years. I was shocked to hear her voice. She didn't ask how I or my son were or how I was coping as a single mum (I'd recently been through a traumatic divorce and the breakdown of my marriage was primarily to do with my family, who had told my husband lies about me, to cover their shame) and she didn't ask if I needed any help as I was unemployed and struggling to make ends meet. She simply said in a cold voice, 'Your mother has just been diagnosed with bowel cancer and it's your duty, as her daughter, to contact her.'

I hung up on my aunt, incensed that she would dare suggest that I speak to my mother after all she'd done. I went into the kitchen, and I was angrily talking out aloud to God saying, 'How dare she tell me my mother is dying, why would I care, my mother killed me years ago, but I didn't have the privilege of dying, instead I've had to live with the pain' and I went on and on and on spilling out years of self-pity, hurt and pain to God.

But what happened next shook me to the core and changed my life forever. Suddenly a huge ceramic pot containing a large vine that had been hanging securely from the ceiling for the last 12 years came smashing down onto the draining board, breaking the vine into pieces. There was soil, ceramic and broken pieces of plant everywhere... This stopped me in my tracks and as I looked at the floor, I saw that a book had fallen from the bookshelf and landed in the middle of the kitchen floor... It was a little book by John and Carol Arnot called 'The Importance of Forgiveness'. I froze as I looked at the book and God spoke to me very clearly. He said, '*Unless you learn to forgive, your life, also, like this vine, will be destroyed.*'

I immediately fell to my knees and sobbed uncontrollably asking for God's forgiveness. It suddenly became so clear to me that the only person I had really sinned against was God and the thought of destroying my relationship with Him now was too much to bear. I asked God to please help me to forgive my mother because I didn't know how to... Immediately the room was filled with peace and the turmoil within me stilled. Twenty minutes later, for the first time in many years I received the grace to calmly telephone my mother and tell her how sorry I was to hear of her diagnosis. This in itself was a miracle.

She said that she was scared and that she needed me because she didn't want to go through this alone. That was the first time in my life I remember my mother wanting to spend time with me.

In a nutshell, I became my mother's full-time carer from diagnosis to death. From that day onwards, my mother went through every gruelling procedure and operation with me by her side and she became dependent on me to wash, feed and take care of her. We had eight months together and we became great friends. She knew that I loved her and that I'd forgiven her, and she died in peace.

Throughout those eight months, God miraculously healed my heart and emotions, He took away the hurt, the pain and the wounding, He took the anger and disappointment, the betrayal and lies. He took the neglect, abandonment and the mental and emotional abuse and I was no longer tortured by my past... What the devil meant for evil, God turned around for good: God restored to me a peace that passes understanding and from that day onwards, He opened doors of blessing and favour into my life that I'd never previously dreamed or imagined possible. He gave me hope for the future and healed my broken heart, but the key to my freedom was the key of forgiveness and I had to personally choose to put that key in the lock – nobody else could do it for me.

I am absolutely convinced that had I chosen *not* to forgive, in God's own words, 'my life like that vine would have been destroyed' and my story today would be very different.

Let me say again, and Sharon's story illustrates this beautifully, that the very act of forgiving someone for what they have done to us forces the devil to remove his foot from the door of our lives, with the result that he can now no longer influence or afflict us. Remember that in the previous chapter, I explained what a foothold is – as long as he has his foot in the door, that open crack allows him access and you can be sure he will take advantage. He is no gentleman! Paul the apostle reminds us of this in 2 Corinthians 2:10–11: 'what I have forgiven – if there was anything to forgive – I have forgiven in the sight of Christ for your sake, in order that Satan might not outwit us. For we are not unaware of his schemes.' Failing to forgive is clearly linked to the devil's schemes in attempting to catch us out.

In my experience, we have often only partially understood the full nature of forgiveness, and it's my intention now to perhaps bring a little clarity to the subject by clearing up a few misunderstandings regarding what forgiveness is *not*.

- Forgiveness is never saying that the wrongdoing was OK. This is probably the greatest hurdle for us in being able to freely forgive others, because it feels to us like the act of forgiving is tantamount to saying that the crime or event wasn't wrong. God never ever says that in forgiving, the person who hurt you is being let off the hook, or that what was done or said to you was not really all that bad. Forgiveness does not condone wrongful actions or words.

- Forgiveness does not mean that you will forget about the event, or the words spoken. In my experience and hearing this from others, the memory will, with time, fade and lose its potency and cutting edge. The pain recedes, and there will come a day when you can think about the occurrence or the person without the evocation of a sense of injustice and injury.

- Forgiveness does not require you to be in communication with the person who has harmed you. God does not ask that of you.

- Forgiveness does not mean that you must continue to tolerate ongoing abuse, of any kind. Sometimes, alongside the willingness to forgive, it might be necessary to involve the police – society demands that crimes be paid for. Nor does forgiving someone mean that you must stay in an abusive or violent relationship. That, too, is not God's desire or intention in asking us to forgive.

- Forgiveness is not taking revenge. The Bible clearly teaches that God will be the avenger. Paul tells us this in Romans 12:18–20: 'If it is possible, as far as it depends on you, live at peace with everyone. Do not take revenge, my dear friends, but leave room for God's wrath, for it is written: "It is mine to avenge; I will repay," says the Lord.'

- Forgiving someone does not mean going to the person and telling them that you have forgiven them, although that might indeed be the right thing to do.

- Forgiveness is not waiting until we receive an apology before extending our forgiveness to those who have hurt us. If we wait for remorse in the other, we might never have the opportunity to forgive. God asks us to forgive our fellow human beings regardless of whether they are aware of having hurt us, or not!

Jesus was punished for us – for every wrong thought, act or words spoken that we have committed knowingly or unknowingly in the past and in the present, and for those we may commit in the future. He was punished once, on the cross 2,000 years ago, and for all of us: 'God made him who had no sin to be sin for us, so that in him we might become the righteousness of God' (2 Corinthians 5:21).

If something hard has happened to you, you need to know that that *is not God punishing you*. Sometimes we feel as though the crime committed against us is justified because we regard it as just punishment for our own past wrongdoing. We therefore do not see the need for forgiveness, but I do not believe that this way of thinking is Biblically correct. For those of us who are His children, we will not be punished for our wrongdoings. In 1 John 4:18 (ESV) we read, 'There is no fear in love, but perfect love casts out fear. For fear has to do with punishment, and whoever fears has not been perfected in love.' *God is not our judge – He is our Father.*

I would like now to explore what forgiveness is, and this might help us to further see why God places such a very high premium on it.

- Forgiveness is a matter between you and God. It has less to do with you and the person who has hurt you, and much more to do with what's going on in your relationship with God. It is a spiritual matter that, if applied to our broken and hurting relationships, ultimately brings greater intimacy with Abba Father. When we refuse to forgive, we will undoubtedly mar our communion with God. No matter how grievously we might have been treated or how badly we are hurting, if we want a deep and genuine connection with God, we have to choose to forgive our fellow human beings. This choice frees us from spiritual bondage. Neil Anderson puts it like this: 'Let him or her off your hook because as long as you refuse to forgive someone, you are still hooked to that person. You are still chained to your past, bound up in your bitterness.'[12] Forgiveness allows the wound to

12 Neil Anderson, *The Bondage Breaker: Interactive Workbook* (Eugene, OR: Hay House, 2011), p. 72.

heal, and the continuing pain can at last begin to ease. It has been said that choosing *not* to forgive is like taking poison in the hope that the other person dies.

- Forgiveness is a choice. It does not come naturally or easily; in fact, the demons will do all in their power to dissuade you from forgiving anyone, ever. We must often grit our teeth and, through clenched jaws, *choose* to forgive. It is a commandment from God that has consequences for us, as we well know from our recitation of the Lord's Prayer: 'forgive us our sins *as* we forgive others'.

- Forgiveness may well mean that we must live with the effects of the other person's behaviour, and that can be devastatingly hard for us, but nonetheless we will still have to live with it, either in peace or in rage. The choice is ours.

After a long shift at the fire department, Matt Swatzell fell asleep while driving and crashed into another vehicle, taking the life of pregnant mother June Fitzgerald and injuring her 19-month-old daughter. Fitzgerald's husband, a full-time pastor, asked for the man's sentence to be diminished, and began meeting with Swatzell for coffee and conversation. Many years later, the two men remain close. 'You forgive as you've been forgiven,' Fitzgerald told *Today*. 'This has been just as healing for me too,' he continued. 'I've taught on forgiveness, and I know that forgiveness is not so much for the other person but for yourself.'[13]

---

13 www.rd.com/list/inspiring-forgiveness-stories

I have been asked, as Peter asked Jesus: 'How many times should I forgive?', and the answer has to be, 'As many times as it takes.' Jesus' reply was 'seventy times seven' (see Matthew 18:21–22). Clearly, forgiveness is not to be meted out in a limited fashion but is to be abundant, overflowing, and available to all, just as the measureless grace of God is poured out upon us. We start with one intentional step, 'I choose to forgive', and see where it takes us. We may need to go there again, and again, and again. But one day, the memory of the event or the person will have no significant emotion attached to it and we will know we are free! And what a truly glorious freedom that is!

- Forgiveness can also manifest itself in our bodies. It seems, from recent studies, that choosing to hang on to bitterness and judgement against another can even affect our physical strength.

  Researchers at Erasmus University in the Netherlands asked people to write about a time when they either gave or withheld forgiveness. The human guinea pigs were then asked to jump as high as they could, five times, without bending their knees. The forgivers jumped highest, about 11.8 inches on average, while the grudge holders jumped 8.5 inches – a huge difference, and a startling illustration of how forgiveness can physically unburden you![14]

14 Originally published in *Readers Digest*, 18 April 2016.

- Forgiveness, finally, also means recognising that we have sat in the seat of judgement during these past weeks, months and years while we have borne our grudges, savoured our hatred and imagined revenge. And yet, God alone can judge humankind because He alone is without sin. So, now it is time to offer mercy to those who have betrayed us and let us down, just as Jesus has been merciful towards us.

I have discussed, at some length, why forgiving others is so very important. It also needs to be said that, quite often, we need to forgive ourselves for the stupid choices and decisions that we have made, sometimes resulting in dire consequences. As with forgiving others, it may seem too easy to simply release ourselves from the hook in this way. It may feel more appropriate to continue to punish ourselves by withholding self-forgiveness. However, in so doing, what we are really saying is that Jesus' sacrifice wasn't enough – that somehow it was inadequate and does not satisfactorily deal with our sin. If God can remove sin from us, as far as the east is from the west, then let's ask ourselves the question, 'Who am I to continue to hold it so close?' (See Psalm 103:12, 'as far as the east is from the west, so far has he removed our transgressions from us').

And finally, sometimes we may need to forgive God if we feel He has let us down or betrayed us or disappointed us in some way. We are not ever saying that He has done anything wrong, because we know that He is without sin, and that He is perfect and loving in all His dealings with us. But we may need to forgive God, perhaps, in order to let go of negative feelings that we are holding against Him. God's shoulders are broad, and He understands us and our reasoning better than we do!

* * *

In the highly acclaimed film *The Railway Man*, based on a true Second World War story, we meet Eric Lomax, a British officer, who is captured by the Japanese in Singapore and sent to a POW camp, where he is forced to work building the Thai–Burma Railway north of the Malay Peninsula. During his time in the camp, Lomax is brutally tortured by the Kempeitai, the military secret police, for building a radio receiver from spare parts. His Japanese captors believe him to be a British spy, but in fact his only intention had been to attempt to listen to the BBC news as a morale booster for himself and his fellow prisoners. Lomax and his surviving comrades are finally rescued by the British Army.

As the film opens, it soon becomes obvious that some 30 years later, Lomax is still suffering the psychological trauma of his wartime experiences, along with the regular occurrence of horrific nightmares. From a newspaper cutting, he discovers that the Japanese secret police officer Takashi Nagase, having escaped prosecution for his war crimes, is now working as a tourist guide in the very camp, now a museum, where he and his men once tortured British POWs. Lomax decides to travel alone to Thailand and returns to the scene of his torture to confront Nagase 'in an attempt to let go of a lifetime of bitterness and hate'. His intentions are clear – to kill or at least to maim Nagase, but he is unable to do so.

After some time, Lomax returns to Thailand, with Patti, his wife. He meets up with Nagase once again and, in an emotional scene, after exchanging and accepting each other's forgiveness, the two make peace, choosing to put the past behind them. The epilogue relates that from then on, Lomax's nightmares gradually ceased, and in fact Nagase and Eric remained friends until their deaths in 2011 and 2012, respectively. Wow!

This film beautifully portrays the power of forgiveness, even from horrendous abuse. At one point Lomax states that 'the hating has to stop'. His decision to forgive not only releases and heals him from the effects of the systematic torture, but also empowers him to move from being a victim to being a survivor and, ultimately, an overcomer.

I urge you, friends, to take time to seriously consider whether there are people in your lives that God is gently reminding you to forgive. He understands the cost to you to do so. He feels with you in your struggle to exonerate another. He sees the inner wrestling that accompanies such a decision. God the Father experienced the agonies of Jesus, and those extraordinary final words from the cross echo through history and stand as a stark reminder of what is right and what is possible: 'Father, forgive them, for they do not know what they are doing' (Luke 23:34).

PAUSE FOR REFLECTION

1. Reread Matthew 18:21–35. What might being 'handed over to be tortured' look like in your life?

2. In this parable, it is money that is owed. You, similarly, may have been robbed of something. Are there people that you need to forgive? What stops you from doing so?

3. We may want mercy for ourselves, but judgement for others. Is this true for you?

If you struggle to find the words to use to forgive others, the following short, simple and yet powerful prayer may be helpful; insert details to fit your own situation. Don't rush this process.

Father God, today I choose to forgive [Jo] for [bullying] me, which made me feel [small and inadequate]. (Be really honest)

Please forgive me for holding [Jo] in judgement and for withholding mercy.

I now choose to bless [Jo] and I release [Jo] to you.

Thank you for my freedom.

Amen

5

WHO AM I?

*Who are we but the stories we tell ourselves, about ourselves,
and believe?*
SCOTT TUROW

Who am I? Who are you? And does it matter what you think
about yourself, how you define yourself?

Who am I? I wonder if you have ever asked yourself the
question. I hadn't. Not in my 50 years of life had I ever asked,
let alone answered, that question.

It's quite an interesting one to consider. If somebody was to
genuinely ask you it, think about how you might answer. Steve
Goss from Freedom in Christ Ministries makes the following
helpful suggestions that we might ponder on the quest to reach
a conclusion.

He starts off by making the point that we are not our names. I could change my name by deed poll, tonight, online, pay £15, and hey presto, wake up tomorrow morning as Belinda Bellamy.

I am *not* my name.

We are not our jobs. I trained as a nurse many years ago, worked on and off in different medical capacities, and finally gave up altogether when we adopted Phoebe. Did I then cease to be me? Did my brother cease to be him when he retired from working in a bank at the age of 58? Of course not.

I am *not* my job.

We are not our physical bodies either. If you were to lose your limbs in a horrible accident, if you donated a lung or a kidney, if you became paralysed from the neck down, would you cease to be you?

I am *not* my physical body.

Nor are you defined by your gifting, or by the wonderful things you do for God. One day you will not have the strength or capacity for these things anymore, but you will still be you.

I am *not* my gifting.

Does my place of birth, my culture or my family of origin

define me? My religious convictions, my political leanings? As powerful as these sometimes are in shaping and moulding us, they carry little weight here.

My sexual orientation does not define me. It is only one expression of the hugely complex and superbly crafted being that I am, and still we have not answered the perplexing question: who am I? The answer has baffled humankind for millennia. We have sought to define ourselves in myriad ways, and most of these leave us with the uncomfortable feeling that this is still not quite it.

So, who am I?

The Bible says, in Psalm 139:13, 'you created my inmost being; you knit me together in my mother's womb.' God created you and me. He uniquely designed us and gave us life, leaving an imprint of Himself within each of us: 'So God created mankind in his own image, in the image of God he created them; male and female he created them' (Genesis 1:27).

To find the answer to our question, we need to see what God says about us. The Bible states: 'to all who did receive him, who believed in his name, he gave the right to become children of God' (John 1:12 ESV). It's important to note that He gives us the right to actually *become* His children, not merely that we *be called* God's children. Later in the New Testament we read this: 'See what kind of love the Father has given to us, that we should be called children of God; *and so we are*' (1 John

3:1 ESV, italics mine). Finally, Paul, writing to the church in Rome, says, 'The Spirit you received does not make you slaves, so that you live in fear again; rather, the Spirit you received brought about your adoption to sonship [i.e., your adoption as sons and daughters].' (Romans 8:15)

I have quoted three verses among many. From God's point of view, the resounding answer to the question of our identity, 'Who am I?', is that we are very definitely children of God. We are His sons and daughters. That is who we are. In earlier chapters, we explored the idea that God is relational and has invited us into a parent/child relationship. He longs for us to relate to Him as Father – and, of course, by definition, that means that we must be His children!

Listen to God speaking to His people Israel through the prophet Jeremiah:

> I myself said,
>> 'How gladly would I treat you like my children
>> and give you a pleasant land,
>> the most beautiful inheritance of any nation.'
> I thought you would call me 'Father'
> and not turn away from following me.
>
> (Jeremiah 3:19)

From the words of John 1:12 (quoted above), 'to all who did receive him, who believed in his name, he gave the right to become children of God', it seems to me that there was a time when we were *not* His sons and daughters. I became a Christian on July 31st, 1982. On that day, in surrendering my life to Jesus, God gave me the right to become His daughter. This then leads me to wonder about who or what I was the day before, on July 30th! Some of you may not be able to put a start date to your faith journey. Nonetheless, however young you might have been, however beautifully simple and naive receiving Jesus might have looked like for you as a small child, I think there will still have been a 'before' and an 'after'.

In a natural and literal sense, the opposite to being a son or a daughter is being an orphan, and this applies spiritually too. The opposite of a son or daughter of God must be an orphan, and the Bible does indeed say this. But we, who have received Jesus are *not* then orphans. In John 14:18, Jesus Himself says, 'I will not leave you as orphans; I will come to you.'

His coming to us changes everything. Our status, our profile, our identity changes. And remember, Jesus says that He is the exact representation of the Father, so 'I won't leave you as orphans' are the Father's words to us. He won't leave us as orphans because He gives us the right to become His children, adopted into His family. So, it seems that until we 'believed in His name', you could say that we were spiritual orphans. On July 30th, 1982, I was an orphan. On July 31st, 1982, I became God's daughter, adopted into a worldwide, gloriously diverse family. Uniquely set apart, all of us culturally, socially, stunningly different, and yet deeply united in Jesus.

On November 29th, 2004, little Lin Kaijuan, now Phoebe, ceased to be an orphan and *became* our daughter. We came to her; we found her where she was. On that hot and humid day, in a functional and formal little handing-over ceremony, we signed the necessary paperwork and received Phoebe into our family. It all happened quickly, efficiently, easily. In an instant. One minute an orphan and the next minute, our daughter. In a moment in time, her identity changed. At 11:00 that morning she had been an orphan and at 11.02 she became our daughter, and nothing can change that – ever. Nothing. Phoebe can choose to leave the protection and provision, the security and love of our home and family, and go away. She would still be our daughter. She can choose to believe, or not believe, that we love her completely and unconditionally, as we do our three birth children. Whatever she thinks or feels, or does, she is still our daughter, and nothing changes that, ever.

And so it is with us and our new identity. No matter how we feel, no matter what happens in our lives, no matter where we have been or where we go, God is our Abba daddy – and we are His sons and daughters, by adoption.

'Adoption in New Testament Times' by Baina David King notes that 'Paul in Galatians [3:26 – 4:6] speaks clearly about the analogy of our spiritual adoption into the family of God'. The author observes that this is indeed 'a beautiful metaphor because it describes the true state of orphans' in the culture of Israel when the apostle was writing:

Just as humanity, living in sin, and without God is hopelessly lost and without hope of ever coming into anything good, so the orphan in the first century world had little to look forward to beyond slavery. When Paul used this as an example of how great the grace of God is to us as believers it must have sent chills down the spines of his readers because the contrast was so great.[15]

One problem that I believe we have is that so often we don't *feel* like sons and daughters, but we are certainly *not* orphans. Back in those long-ago days as a young missionary wife and mum in Pakistan, I didn't feel as if I belonged. I felt insignificant. I didn't feel that I was known and accepted by God, and right through my life until really fairly recently, the all-too-familiar phrase that kept playing in my mind, was 'am I seen? Am I seen?'. I felt as though I was passed over by God. And yet I was a Bible-believing, Spirit-filled Christian. I certainly didn't feel like God's daughter.

I think we probably all have something like this – a refrain, a sense, a feeling, a longing that repeats itself. Sometimes it lies dormant, even for years, and then at other times it is triggered by an event, a memory, a chance meeting. For you, it might be a tendency towards anxiety or fear. Maybe a sense of being rejected, not included, creeps up on you from time to time, or feelings of not being enough, or perhaps, too much,

15 Baina David King, 'Adoption in New Testament Times', Senior Honors Thesis, Liberty University, 2005. https://digitalcommons. liberty.edu/honors/186

seem to follow you around and you can't quite shake it off.

These strong emotions feel so true, but they are not *the* truth. You may have been abandoned or rejected, as Phoebe was, found on a step in Southern China. But the past does not define you. You have been given the right to become a child of God and that is who you are right now. No child of God is abandoned or rejected or a failure or unwanted or dirty or alone.

It is because we don't feel like beloved sons and daughters that we also don't behave as such. Our feelings translate into action, and this looks like something. What we truly believe about ourselves, about God, is seen in the way we live our lives. Oh, we say all the right things – we speak the Christian lingo fluently and are well versed in it. But very often we don't act like children of a good Heavenly Father; we don't live as though the phrases and verses that trip smoothly off our tongues are true. We feel, and behave in fact, more like orphans as though there was no one to care for us, to love us, protect us or provide for us.

If you're an orphan like our daughter Phoebe was, who is your dad and who is your mum? You don't have a mum or a dad. The Oxford dictionary defines the word 'orphan' as 'a child whose parents are dead'.

As an orphan, you are literally on your own in this world and you must look after yourself. When we adopted Phoebe and brought her home to West Yorkshire from Southern China, at 21 months old, we discovered that Phoebe had already learned that she needed to take care of herself because no one else would. She was already potty-trained; she was able to dress herself; she nibbled her own fingernails and toenails to keep them trimmed. Phoebe was a very independent little tot. When she woke in the mornings she did not cry from her cot, ever; she would wait and wait until we came to her. She would have quietly waited for ever. Phoebe has always been mature for her age, and now, as a beautiful 19-year-old, she is very capable, independent and self-sufficient, which in a young adult are admirable qualities. However, to watch her as a toddler, meeting her own needs, was heartbreaking. Her self-reliant ways, as sweet and as endearing as they were in such a small little girl, were the ways of an orphan. Even at that tender age, she had had to learn to look out for herself.

An orphan who grows up never knowing the love of a father, whether biological or adopted, has a very different viewpoint to life and to themselves than that of a son or daughter of loving parents. There is no sense of security, of being protected, of worth, of acceptance and belonging, of being loved and valued.

But you know, we might have loving mums and dads and yet still act as though we are orphans; we can live as though our hearts are orphaned. And likewise, children of God who love Jesus, who have given Him their lives and have been adopted, spiritually, into His family, can still be orphan-hearted, displaying orphan traits in their relationships and in their understanding of the nature of God.

Let's look a little further at these orphan traits and patterns of behaviour that we all tend to display to one degree or another, in spite of being God's sons and daughters and not orphans at all.

Literal orphans, remember, have to fend for themselves. Think of street children in so many of the world's sprawling cities, or children who have been orphaned by war and violence. They have to anticipate and meet their own needs. No one else will do it for them. Orphans are fiercely independent and self-reliant. They have learned to trust no one. This is also evident in spiritual orphans.

People like you and me, we are Bible-believing followers of Jesus, and the Holy Spirit lives in us. Yet we too are guilty of competing in relationships for positions of influence and power. We accuse and criticise others in order to feel good about ourselves. We strive for approval and admiration and acceptance. Often, we are competitive and jealous of the success of others. We are often guarded and conditional in our relationships, and in the way we express love, being wary of vulnerability and exposure. We work hard to cover shame and we try to seek and control our fears. Feelings of low self-esteem and insignificance are very familiar to orphans, who are also, oh, so very easily offended.

Spiritual orphans display these traits because, deep inside, they don't know who they are – their identity is dependent on how others see them, or on performance and achievement. We all know people like this at work, and in our colleges; we bump into them in the shops and come across them on the roads and, dare I say it, in our churches. I think we can also recognise some of these traits *in ourselves*. I could have ticked the whole list in the years when I was grappling with my own issues related to identity. It is an exhausting and an unhappy way to live.

Nobody else may have seen that in me, but I knew in the depths of my being that I was doing all of that. Yet God, who describes himself as our Heavenly Father, says that we are *adopted* into His family. We are not orphans, so why do we live as though we are?

The Bible teaches that when we were born, we were not connected to God. We were born spiritually dead, but physically alive, and then when we met Jesus and realised we needed him, we committed our lives to Him. At that moment we were born again of the Spirit, and that new birth gave us a new identity, whether we were aware of it at the time, or not. Jesus says so in John 3:6–7: 'Flesh gives birth to flesh, but the Spirit gives birth to spirit. You should not be surprised at my saying, "You must be born again."'

In that moment, the old went and the new came and we became children of God, orphans no more. I believe this happens in exactly the same way as it did for Phoebe. Even as the ink was still drying on the freshly signed adoption paperwork, her identity changed – one minute an orphan, and the next, a daughter.

We have said that it is God Himself who defines who He is, and not the stuff that happens to us, or the way we feel. He also defines who *we* are. Who He says we are and the way He thinks about us do not waver, whatever our behaviour, our faults or failings. He is the great unchanging I AM, and what He thinks about us does not change. He is not like us, tossed emotionally this way and that, fickle and unpredictable. Abba Father is consistent in His nature – rocklike and unmovable in His love and affection for us. His character is immutable and steadfast, the only thing in our lives that is constant.

We have learned to see ourselves in a certain way perhaps because of what we have gone through, and due to what 'significant others' have said about us. The culture of our family of origin might have been an encouraging, nurturing environment or a critical, condemning one. But *now* we are children of God. God defines us – we are who He says we are. The much-loved American author, Philip Yancey, says this: 'there is nothing we can do to make God love us more [and] there is nothing we can do to make God love us less.'[16] This is the staggering truth. If I were to choose right now to sit in my chair and do nothing for the rest of my life, God would not, could not, love me any less than if I got up right now and, leaving all that I love behind, set off to Outer Mongolia for Him as a missionary. He loves for love's sake. His love is independent of any effort or attempt on our behalf to be pleasing to Him. You and I please and delight Him today, just as we are, with

16 Philip Yancey, *What's So Amazing about Grace?* (New York: Harper Collins, 1997), p. 70.

no provisos, no caveats, no prerequisites. You are His beloved son, His adored daughter, and His desire is for you (Song of Songs 7:10).

This is very counter-cultural. Western civilization has taught us from day one that performance and productivity will reward us with what we all desperately need and want – namely to be loved and accepted unconditionally, no strings attached – and it fails us. No matter how successful we become, how popular we are, how much we are affirmed, lauded or celebrated, it is never enough.

And here we are now, as His children, with God Himself answering these deep longings in His astonishing and extravagant invitation to father us – if we would only humbly accept Him as the lover of our souls, the refuge in our storms, the light in our darkness, our all, in all.

* * *

Steve and I were sitting on a wall in Cornwall, on holiday, right on the beach – we were captivated, watching a little group of small children playing in the sand. Those three and four-year-olds were immersed in their game, building a haphazard sandcastle, studded with shells, sticks and pebbles, carrying water from the edge of the sea, to and fro, in small, brightly coloured plastic buckets. Absorbed in watching this sweet scenario, the spirit of God whispered to me, 'That's how I want you to live.' With this unexpected invitation came a revelation.

As I chewed over His words, it occurred to me that these little ones didn't have a care in the world. Those tots were not thinking about whether the mortgage or rent had been paid that month. Their thoughts were not taken up with whether mum had remembered to bring ham, and not cheese, sandwiches for lunch, or if there would be enough petrol in the car to get home at the end of the day. Those four-year-olds were not worried about turning five next year and starting school. No – a small child's dependence and reliance on his parents to meet all his needs is complete and total. Our grandson Max is four and I now see how he lives in the moment. He has no cares in the world – he assumes, no, he *expects* that he will be provided for, that he will be protected, that his parents will be able to do anything, anywhere and at any time. To his small, simple way of thinking, Max's mum and dad are without limits in knowledge, ability, understanding and skill. They are for him, aged four, all he needs. They are enough. They are his world. His sweet little adorable life revolves around them entirely. He does not question their decisions, he believes what they tell him, and his trust in them is complete.

The New Testament says this of Jesus: 'He called a little child to him and placed the child among them. And he said: "Truly I tell you, unless you change and become like little children, you will never enter the kingdom of heaven"' (Matthew 18:2–3). When I was first introduced to Jesus and said 'yes' to His invitation, I did so as a child – I did not understand the gospel – I did not then grasp the significance of the cross. I had never opened a Bible. My unquestioning ability at that time to say a resounding 'yes' displayed a simple, childlike faith. Just as Max did when his mum told him he was going on a plane to America, or to London's Great Ormond Street Children's Hospital to have his birthmark lasered. He had no idea what a plane was, or America or a hospital, or laser treatment. His simple but absolute trust in the good nature of his parents was enough and all that was required for him to hold their hands and follow them into the unknown.

I think we probably all started out well on this faith journey, as I did, but now the problem we have is that we have all become so grown up, sophisticated and independent. The Kingdom of God, however, is an upside-down kingdom and I think that God was trying to tell me something profound that day on the beach in Cornwall. His greatest desire is that we all live from day to day displaying the simple faith of a four-year-old, placed in our rock-like Abba Father whose good nature is steadfast and certain.

We will not experience life in all its fullness, joy and adventure, unless we intentionally choose to live as little children, dependent on Abba Father to meet all our needs for acceptance and unconditional love. I believe that it is absolutely possible to live daily as sons and daughters. If we are not approaching every day with an expectation of goodness and kindness from the hand of God and hope in *every* situation, then I think you could say that to some extent, our hearts are orphaned.

My exhausting orphan-ways are diminishing – the internal

dialogue is now much weaker, as I hang on to what He says. I don't have to prove myself to Him or to anyone anymore. I don't have to fight to be heard; I don't have to do stuff and be busy to be significant. I don't have to be considered beautiful or spiritual. I can just be me. He loves me, and He has proved it to me over and over again. What God says and thinks about me is surely more important than anybody else's opinion.

I feel that I need to say, again, at this point, that while reaching that place of freedom from fears and anxieties is our goal, it does not happen overnight, at least certainly not in my experience. The goal is to live daily as beloved sons and daughters, in a loving and dependent relationship with God, knowing Him as a Father who delights in us. However, the journey to this glorious destination is lifelong, and in this age of quick fixes and instant everything, many can't or won't stay the course, slipping permanently back into old habits and former ways of thinking and behaving, because it seems easier than pressing on. Jesus says in Matthew 11:12, and the Amplified Bible expresses it well: 'From the days of John the Baptist until now the kingdom of heaven suffers violent assault, and violent men seize it by force [as a precious prize].'

I do believe there has to be a measure of spiritual violence in grabbing and holding on to these truths. You and I have to really, really want this freedom; we must be willing to go after it, no matter what the cost, no matter how hard the road might be, and in the moment of temptation we must be tenacious and intentional in putting aside old ways, in order to rehearse new, unfamiliar truths. It often seems easier to go with the mantras of 'I'm no good, I can't do this, God doesn't see me, love me, know me', which over years of use have become our friends, than it does to reject these untruths in favour of another narrative, particularly when in the middle of the assault.

Jesus tells us that He came so that we might live full and abundant lives – rich lives of deep connection with one another, free from fear and resting in the embrace of the only One who truly knows and understands us. This is the experience of *sons and daughters*, living securely in their belovedness – not that the road is without its challenges, heartache, or trauma, but that as it is travelled, their hands are tightly held.

Gerald May beautifully echoes my own thoughts:

> I know that God is loving, and that God's loving is trustworthy. I know this directly, through the experience of my life. There have been plenty of times of doubt, especially when I used to believe that trusting God's goodness meant I would not be hurt. But having been hurt quite a bit, I know God's goodness goes deeper than all pleasure and pain. It embraces them both.[17]

---

17 Quoted in Brennan Manning, *Ruthless Trust: The Ragamuffin's Path to God* (New York: HarperOne, 2000), p. 22.

PAUSE FOR REFLECTION

1. What defines you? Does who you think you are matter? Why or why not?

2. Would you say that you live as a secure and beloved child of God? If not, what steps might you want to take in order to begin to see yourself as God sees you, and therefore as you truly are?

3. We all display orphan traits, to one degree or another. Are you aware of any of the following in yourself?

   a. *Fiercely independent*
   b. *Don't easily trust*
   c. *Competitive in relationships*
   d. *Strive for approval, admiration, acceptance*
   e. *Jealous of other people's success*
   f. *Often feel insignificant*
   g. *Struggle with feelings of low self-worth*
   h. *Assume you'll be rejected*
   i. *Other...?*

4. Ask the Holy Spirit to help you identify where you are exhibiting orphan ways. Perhaps take a few quiet moments now to repent of them, asking Father God to forgive you for living as an orphan and not as His beloved child.

6
TRUTH OR LIES?

The truly scary thing about undiscovered lies is that they have a greater
capacity to diminish us than exposed ones.
CHERYL HUGHES

A Sunday school teacher once asked a group of children for their definition of faith. One little boy eagerly raised his hand. 'Faith is trying very, very hard to believe what you know isn't really true!' And yes, sometimes it really feels like that, doesn't it?

We need to look at the subject of faith if we are to understand how to apply Biblical truth to our lives in such a way that it is truly transformative.

What is your definition, I wonder, of the word 'faith'?

It's a word that can be used in many ways and we don't all mean the same thing when using it. We might say, 'I don't have faith for "such and such"', but what do we mean by that? Are we in fact saying that we don't believe God can do 'such and such'?

In what feels like another life, and many years ago, I worked as a nurse in the local hospice. I loved just being there. I loved the calm and the peace, such a soothing environment after the intensity and drama of a ward job in a busy hospital. In those days we had all the time in the world to sit with patients, to attend to their physical needs without rush or compromise. Sitting in comfortable companionship with someone who is facing death is a humbling and often beautiful experience. The conversation, if there was one, often alighted on the subject of religion, and I might gently probe, asking, 'Do you have a faith that comforts you?' What did I mean in asking this, and what was in their mind in answering?

A few of us recently discussed Noah's ark and we all expressed how hard it is for us to get our head around the idea that two badgers, two mosquitos, two lions and two penguins, among hundreds of other creatures and insects, made their way onto the ark from all over the world! It is a fantastical proposition to our evidence-based biased Western mindset! We concluded, however, that as Jesus refers to it as an historical event, and as God raised Him from death, then organising two badgers, two mosquitos, two lions and two penguins to make their way onto the ark was probably possible! Biblical stories such as this one undoubtedly 'stretch' our faith. By that, we are saying that, to our way of thinking, with our twenty-first century understanding of how the world works (which is, as I have already pointed out, conditioned and confirmed by a particular worldview), this event as described in Genesis seems improbable, and even impossible for some of us to believe.

As a side note, it is fascinating to discover that catastrophic flood accounts can be found in many of the world's cultures, appearing in their ancient stories and legends. One of the oldest and most interesting accounts originates in Hindu mythology, dating back to the sixth century BC, and while there are discrepancies, it does bear a fascinating similarity to the Genesis story of Noah and his ark. Likewise, since the dawn of Chinese civilization, some 4,500 years ago, pictographic characters for 'boat' and 'flood' recall information as recounted in the adventures of Noah and his ark-borne family. These Chinese characters record that there were exactly eight survivors of the worldwide flood!

If you have travelled to lands and cultures away from your own, you will have come across some strange and wonderful beliefs that people put their faith in regarding very ordinary life-events. In Japan, black cats are considered lucky, for example, while in England, black cats are considered to bring bad luck. Chinese folk culture is full of advice about foods that pregnant women should avoid: eating crab might make your baby mischievous or give it 11 fingers; drinking milk can lighten its skin; consuming squid might make your womb 'sticky'. In some parts of the developing world, it is still believed that cow dung makes a good poultice for the umbilical cord.

In seeking to explore what we mean by faith, we must remember that our belief systems are, inevitably, moulded and governed from babyhood by the worldview of the prevailing culture, which in turn will ultimately influence and affect our faith in God. It is possible that even as Bible-believing Christians, we don't really know why or what we believe, even though we might also profess that our 'faith' is the most important thing to us.

Faith is the basic ingredient needed to begin a relationship with God. We all employed a measure of faith when we decided to become followers of Jesus. We may not have seen, heard or felt anything tangible, but we had become convinced of the reality of God and our need of a Saviour, and so we took a faith-filled step forward and said 'yes'. In a simple childlike way, we perhaps tentatively, perhaps boldly, said that 'yes', though to our unconvinced family and friends it didn't make sense; it sounded foolish and irrational. But not to us. Not at that moment. Sadly, though, with the passing of time and with all that life has dealt us, that initial strong childlike faith has become a little cynical, more doubting and somewhat dulled. Yes, we would say that we still love Jesus, but our childlikeness has been eroded, partly, perhaps, due to the pervading cultural creeds and ideologies that surround us and continually bombard us.

The Bible tells us that our faith is the assurance that the things revealed and promised in the Word of God are *actually* true, even though unseen. Scripture also gives us, as Christians, a conviction that what we expect, in faith, will come to pass. Therefore, it is vitally important that we decide, once and for all, what our attitude is to the Bible. Will we read it so that therein we might meet Him? Will we choose to read in humility, seeking in its pages the One who created us and completes us? Or is our approach to it clouded by scepticism and unbelief?

Faith is a big deal to God. Faith on an everyday level, faith extended towards God for healing, provision, protection. How often do you have to lean into God with nothing more to go on than His good, good nature? When was the last time He had to come through for you, or else? Hebrews 11:6 tells us that 'without faith it is impossible to please God'.

In our Western culture everything is provided on a plate – education, a healthcare system, benefits, pensions, bus passes for some. We don't have to exercise our faith very much on a day-to-day basis. And then when it comes to emotional or spiritual or psychological needs, we go to the doctor, or we book an appointment with the therapist or the psychologist. We pour our hearts out to our friends or turn to a bottle of wine to dull the pain. It doesn't seem to occur to us that our lack of faith in His ability to father us well grieves the heart of God.

We are never encouraged to struggle or to labour in our relationship with God; rather we are told not to be anxious or fearful – we are to trust God for and with everything. However, there is one passage in the New Testament where we are indeed urged to strive, and it is in the letter to the Hebrews:

> So then, there remains a Sabbath rest for the people of God, for whoever has entered God's rest has also rested from his works as God did from His. Let us therefore *strive* to enter that rest, so that no one may fall by the same sort of disobedience [which is unbelief].
>
> (Hebrews 4:9–11 ESV, italics mine)

Rest here is equated with faith. As long as we are 'working', doing stuff, fixing ourselves and our lives, we are not *resting* in God's ability to sort us out. This is important. When we rest from our works, we move from a place of concern for ourselves and of meeting our needs, to a place of faith, resting in God, on who He is and on what He says, and in His ability to take care of us.

In this do-it-yourself era, when we are encouraged to be independent, and there are self-help books on just about everything, there is only One who knows what we need, who knows how to fix us, and He says to us, 'I know your frame; I remember that you are dust' (see Psalm 103:14).

Because of busyness, and chaos, we don't still ourselves, and often it is because we don't like what we see and hear in that stillness. Some of us hide our pain by our activity; for some of us, our egos are fed by our responsibilities, commitments and busyness. Others want to be seen to be involved, but God is not deceived. He sees our hearts.

In the stillness, before God, He whispers to us to 'let go', and that is hard to do when we have lived so long with our coping strategies and, dare I say it, metaphorically, with our masks!

So, rest is an issue of faith, and faith is a matter of relationship. In whom are we putting our faith? In whom must we rest? Can God be trusted? Truly trusted? What will happen if we let go? If we stop? If we take Him at His word?

Once we decide that God is to be trusted, that what He says is truth, our responsibility is then to believe His words. It is incumbent upon us to do so. Hebrews 11:1 (ESV) says this: 'Now faith is the assurance of things hoped for, the conviction of things not seen.' So, unlike the answer given by the Sunday school child that I referred to earlier on, for us as Christians, faith is choosing to believe what we already know is true, because God has said it, and He doesn't lie. It has little to do with what things feel like or look like in the natural, physical world around us. In the absence of sight or feelings, we must choose to believe that God heals, that He will take care of us, that He will provide for us in a time of financial need. Because He says He will.

This past week has been hard for me – the effects of Covid and an accumulation of disappointment and some sadness had left me feeling empty and at the end of myself. I shared my state of mind with my friend for her prayers, and she replied, with such confidence, 'I am praying for your breakthrough, which will most certainly come. I know it will because it says so in Psalm 145.' The passage she was referring to is this:

You draw near to those who call out to you,
  listening closely, especially when their hearts are true.
Every godly one receives
  even more than what they ask for.
For you hear what their hearts really long for,
  and you bring them your saving strength.
God, you watch carefully over all your devoted lovers like a
  bodyguard...

(Psalm 145:18–20 TPT)

Now, what will I do with this? Do I choose faith or cynicism? Belief or unbelief? Can I, will I, apply these stunning, yet ancient words of hope and comfort to myself and to my current situation, now, in the twenty-first century? The choice is mine, and what I choose will ultimately determine my outlook, my experience and my peace or lack of it in the coming days.

I make the decision to take those words for myself, today, to take hope from them in my unique situation. My faith in God as my Abba daddy compels me to take them at face value and claim them as my own. I declare them over myself and thank Him for His love, for what He will do, for the breakthrough that is one day coming my way. I choose to ignore the present flatness and the fragility of my heart, and I hang on to the promises that He speaks to those like me, who today are broken-hearted. It will not always be like this. With God nothing is impossible, and He has not forgotten us.

I believe, no, I *know*, that faith does have the capacity to move us from this place of being stuck in hopelessness to that of possibility and hope. By faith, we can truly overcome as He overcame: 'for everyone born of God overcomes the world. This is the victory that has overcome the world, even our faith' (1 John 5:4).

I believe that the issue of faith is extremely important to God. I think that some of the saddest words expressed by Jesus were probably those found in Luke 18:8. He is speaking to his followers, encouraging them to be persistent in prayer and not to lose heart, and then He says, perhaps longingly, 'Nevertheless, when the Son of Man comes, will he find faith on earth?' (ESV).

Biblical faith, like hope, discussed in an earlier chapter, is only possible because of the nature and character of God. If our picture of God is skewed, then, as Christians, we will not have a strong robust place from which to start to exercise our faith. So here we are again, back to the question I posed at the beginning of the book, 'Who is God?'. I will ask again: is He that old man with a white beard up in the sky somewhere – a nice ol' guy, but pretty ineffective when it comes to what's going on down here? On the other hand, perhaps He is a strict and harsh headteacher type of character, with a little stick, waiting for you to trip up? Maybe the image is more of an amazing, incredible Creator, but oh so very busy running the universe with no time for your little concerns. Or is He some sort of a control freak ruining all your fun, insisting that you live according to His rules?

I remember being in Pakistan as that young missionary wife and mother. The sense of having been abandoned by God felt so strong. I did all I could in my power to make the feeling go away. I repented of everything and anything I could possibly think of that I might have done wrong or had failed to do. Weeping, and crying out to God, I was unable to find solace or comfort for my deeply hurting heart. I even ripped my Bible from cover to cover in anger and frustration! I had taken offence at God, but God is God, and He did not owe me anything. Jesus says in Matthew 11:6, 'blessed is the one who is not offended by me.' He knows He will offend us, intellectually, emotionally and spiritually. But really, we are only offended because we are so often arrogant and proud and think we know what's best, and because we do not fully trust Him and His ways.

During that time, every day I diligently read my Bible. However, I spent far more time meditating on the word of the enemy than I did meditating on the Word of God because the words and thoughts swirling around my mind felt truer to me than what I read. I didn't know then what I know now – that in agreeing with these lies I was empowering the demons behind them. I didn't know then that I would never really be free as long as I chose to believe the lies. Remember Jesus' words about the enemy: 'there is no truth in him. When he lies, he speaks his native language, for he is a liar and the father of lies' (John 8:44).

What are the thoughts in your head about yourself? A well-known speaker says this: 'You cannot afford to think anything about yourself that God is *not* thinking about you.' I think he's right. Not every thought that enters your head is to be trusted, especially when it speaks to your identity or to God's identity. That's the clue. Thoughts that bring into question whether you are His beloved child or whether God is a good father, come from the pit of hell.

I have already said that we are all in a battle, whether we like it or not, whether we want to acknowledge it or not, and that we can't afford to be apathetic about this aspect of our lives as Christians. The battlefield itself is not, of course, in a physical place, because the battle here that we are discussing is not a physical one – it is a spiritual one. The battlefield is our mind.

Take an act of terror, for example. All actions, whether for good or for evil, start with a thought in our minds. The thought might be vague and nebulous to begin with, but as it is given attention it takes shape. It is now an idea. It is chewed on and mulled over and eventually shared with others. As it gains traction, action is taken and then, one day, a bomb explodes, and lives are lost. What resulted in bloodshed, loss and terror, started as a formless concept. Everything starts in the mind. However, just because a thought flits into our consciousness doesn't mean we have to grab it and hold on to it and agree with it. We can be selective, and we can determine which thoughts are worthy of our attention as God's sons and daughters, and which are nonsense and must be rejected. Immediately.

In the previous chapter we began to look at what we really

think about ourselves. Who are we? We concluded that what God says is what counts and He calls those who believe in His name, sons and daughters. And yet, so often we don't feel like children of a loving Heavenly Father, and many times we certainly don't act like God's beloved children. We feel, and behave in fact, more like orphans with no one to care for us, love us, protect us or provide for us. For many of us, like me in Pakistan, our heads are full of lies, and sometimes our whole personality has developed and is defined by them. We think they protect us, but what the lies do is keep us from really knowing the love of our Heavenly Father. They serve to keep us away from Him, and they blind us to the truth. Their very existence prohibits us from coming close, from intimacy with God. Because of lies, the voice of the Good Shepherd is less easily discernible, and we cannot hear Him so clearly. It is therefore harder to stay deeply connected to God, and the lies most definitely hold us back from fully trusting Him, as much as we would so often like to.

The jottings in my journals from 1995, 1996 and 1997 are testimony to this fact. While on the one hand, they document a very honest and raw account of my thoughts and feelings at the time, their frankness also exposes the extent to which, even as a child of God, I was being tossed this way and that by untruths.

And yes, I was very vulnerable at that time, and yes, I had a lot to cope with. But *no*, I was not worthless. *No*, I was not a useless person. *No*, God had not passed me by. *No*, God had not left me, and *no*, God had not ceased to care about me.

The BABCP website describes Cognitive Behavioural Therapy (CBT) in this way:

> Cognitive Behavioural Therapy is a family of talking therapies, all based on the idea that thoughts, feelings, what we do, and how our bodies feel, are all connected. If we change one of these, we can alter all the others. When we're low or upset, we often fall into patterns of thinking and responding which can worsen how we feel. CBT works to help us notice and change problematic thinking styles or behaviour patterns so we can feel better.[18]

Where have we heard something like this before? Written in the Old Testament sometime between the tenth and sixth centuries BC, Proverbs 23:7 (KJV) reminds us that, 'as [a man] thinketh in his heart, so is he'. This is profound! What we think, and what we believe deep down, determines the sort of people we believe we are, and consequently, how we will behave in any given situation. How we show up out there on the sports field, how we behave when we face conflict with our peers in college, or our emotional response to being let down by a friend are all determined by who we believe we are. Steve Goss, from Freedom in Christ ministry, emphasises this well. He says this: 'You don't feel your way into good behaviour – you behave your way into good feelings. Start by making a choice to believe the truth. Your feelings will follow in due course.' [19]

---

18 The British Association for Behavioural and Cognitive Psychotherapies.
19 Neil T. Anderson & Steve Goss, "Freedom in Christ" Discipleship Course, Published by Lion Hudson Ltd, 2017 p. 40.

We have identified in an earlier chapter that lies originate in the kingdom of darkness. Remember that Jesus Himself said of the devil, 'There is no truth in him. When he lies, he speaks his native language, for he is a liar and the father of lies.' But what about the truth? The world around us is full of opposing narratives, and the voices that relentlessly confront us, day in and day out, are often loud and aggressive, antithetical and contradictory. So, what is truth?

In John's Gospel, Jesus, speaking of Himself as the shepherd, and about us as His sheep, makes this statement:

> The sheep hear his voice, and he calls his own sheep by name and leads them out. When he has brought out all his own, he goes before them, and the sheep follow him, for they know his voice. A stranger they will not follow, but they will flee from him, for they do not know the voice of strangers.
>
> (John 10:3–5 ESV)

Jesus seems so confident, doesn't he? So sure that we, His beloved sheep, will only listen to His voice, that we won't be distracted, manipulated or deceived by the voice of the stranger.

We know that everybody in the world suffers somehow, at some time or another – some more, *way* more than others – but we all experience suffering. The adversity itself, however, is not really the problem. Put simply, the devil will take any opportunity he can, to begin to whisper lies to us, in response to a tragedy, a crisis, a health scare or a financial concern. He does not care whether we are two or 102 years old. The difficulty begins with what we then start to believe. Whose words will we heed? Is it the Good Shepherd's voice, speaking words of comfort and hope, or is it the voice of the stranger, accusing and whining? Therein lies the real issue.

I mentioned in chapter three that the devil does not have a creative bone in his body – the lies that he tempts us to believe are the same old ones that he whispered to Eve in the garden, and, surprise, surprise, they are no different from those with which he tried to entice Jesus in the wilderness after His baptism. Ultimately, the lies will always be aimed at causing us to doubt God's goodness and His intentions towards us, which inevitably result in us querying the depth of God's love for us. He plays mental games, manipulating God's word and twisting the truth, causing confusion and mistrust. From the beginning, the devil intended that human beings should decide for themselves what is good and what is evil. By sowing the seed that God was unreasonable, Eve, who had known nothing but the bounty and goodness of God, fell for the cunning trick, and we too continue to succumb to it today!

'Did God really say, "You must not eat from any tree in the garden"?', asked the devil (Genesis 3:1). Or in other words, 'Surely not! He wouldn't say that! He wants you to prosper and enjoy life; He wouldn't withhold anything from you or want you to go without.' Of course, there are innumerable variations on this theme: *If God cared for me, this would not have happened. If God really loved me, I would not be in this mess...* But essentially, they all call into doubt God's goodness and His love for us, the result of which leads us to pass judgement on His word.

Those who have found CBT to be useful learn how to help themselves shift from a negative mindset to a more positive frame of mind. As Christians, however, we understand from the Bible that this alone is not the solution in the long run. When I was battling with depression, part of the problem for me was that the consistently negative pattern of thinking that I rehearsed in my mind was, as far as I could see it, the truth. I really was useless, and a disappointment to God. He absolutely was not interested in me. I most definitely was 'less than' others. I was unable, at that time, to distinguish lies from truth. On an intellectual level, I agreed with what I read in my daily Bible readings, but my heart was experiencing something altogether different.

In the core of our being we have a deep and visceral desire to be known, to belong, to be significant. When you know in the deepest part of you that, no matter where you have been, what you have done or failed to do, you are unconditionally loved and accepted, those primordial longings in your heart are met. Only God loves like this. Only God's love is pure and perfect. Only God's love completes us and makes us whole. Only God's love provides the solution to our distress. Lies lodged deep in our hearts, sometimes from childhood, cloud our ability to accept this extraordinary love. They form, as it were, a barrier that gets in the way of seeing and understanding truth.

Jesus said of Himself, 'I am the way and the truth and the life.' Because in very essence He *is* the truth, rather than merely *teaching* truth, His words, His thoughts and His actions must all reveal truth to us. Truth, therefore, is not an idea, an ideology or an abstract concept. Truth is a person. Jesus.

Martin Luther King Jr said these words: 'Don't tell me what you believe; show me what you do, and I'll tell you what you believe.' That was me. I could see that what I said I believed, and what I read in my Bible, did not match how I lived and experienced life. There was an incongruity that I had no idea how to tackle. A gap I could not bridge. Something was wrong and I did not know how to deconstruct my obviously faulty perceptions.

We returned from six years in Pakistan with our tail between our legs, so to speak. Broken. Disappointed. Sad. I was tired, spiritually dry and desperate for God, and for the reality of His presence. I was worn out from striving to get Him to be who I thought I needed Him to be. And in this place, along the way, at some point – I can't even remember when – I learned something really important. I came to understand that there are some things that are God's responsibility and there are some things that are our responsibility. The Bible says that God 'has granted to us everything pertaining to life and godliness' (2 Peter 1:3 NASB). *Everything*. For *life* and *godliness*. That means He cannot give us anything else, that there is no more He can do for us. He has done it all. It is finished.

So, while I wept and wrestled with God, pleading for Him to 'do something', unbeknown to me, He had already done it! This takes us back to faith. Remember I said that I believe that faith has within itself the capacity to move us from this place of being stuck, to that place of possibility, and hope? Well, herein lies the key. Everything God has given us for life and godliness is appropriated by faith, and so, by choosing to believe God's word and do what it tells us to do, what will eventually ensue will be the abundant life that Jesus promises. This then is our responsibility – to do what He tells us to do. To believe what He says. It doesn't work to simply ask God to take insecurity away, take anxiety away, take fear away, as in: 'Please God, make me feel better about myself.' I think He watches us and hears our cries with deep sorrow and compassion, and maybe a little frustration. He has given us the tools, He has given us the authority, He has given us His Spirit; the devil is a crushed worm beneath our feet with no power over us. What else can God do? He stands by, cheering us on as our greatest encourager, willing us to follow His instructions.

CBT is great in many ways, but for us as Christians it does not consider the ways of the devil. We can declare good things about ourselves and about our lives, but unless we break the power that the lies have over us, they will continue to exert a certain amount of control. Long, long before CBT was ever invented, Paul the apostle wrote: 'We demolish arguments and every pretension [*every lie*] that sets itself up against the knowledge of God [*what we know to be true of God*], and we take captive every thought to make it obedient to Christ' (2 Corinthians 10:5, italics mine).

To demolish, to take captive – these are violent and aggressive action words. A certain amount of spiritual brute force and fervour is required in the pulling down of lies and in the rebuilding of truth in their place; a tenacity and a single-mindedness is needed. As I have said before, we cannot afford to be apathetic, passive or indifferent. We are all engaged in a battle.

We must decimate the lies, choose truth, and believe that we have what we need, by faith, and then we must begin to walk in it. This is our mandate. This is our responsibility. This is our calling. So that the world out there might know and see the Church victorious, a testimony to full and healed lives, expressed abundantly, in Jesus.

We are all prone to believing lies. Maybe not all the time; maybe they surface when things are not going so well for us, or when we hit a crisis, or our dreams are dashed. The very, very good news is that we can get rid of the lies by breaking our agreement with them. Because the devil is the father of lies, it's as if there is a little demonic critter attached to the ungodly beliefs that we believe. In severing our mental assent to the lie, we disempower the critter and cut ourselves off from the source of the lie. With the power now gone, by speaking truth over ourselves and by making the choice to believe it, we can begin to change the habit that we have developed of defaulting to that particular lie.

Jesus, in Luke 10:19 (ESV), says: 'I have given you authority … over all the power of the enemy'. Come on, friends, we can do this – let's not allow ourselves to be lied to, and stolen from, any longer! Enough is enough!

As for me, I look back with some sadness at all the years spoiled and damaged by believing lies, by doubting God's word and by allowing feelings and circumstances to rule and dictate to me. But I am also supremely grateful that God has shown me these things and has helped me to understand that it is really possible to live victoriously, day by day, no matter what life throws at me.

Identity truly is the key to freedom. If we all had the correct Biblical understanding of God as our wonderful Abba, ourselves as His beloved, and our enemy for the defeated worm that he is, then just imagine what the worldwide church would look like. If we lived wholeheartedly according to the truth as revealed in Jesus, we would offer something so precious and so desperately needed by a broken and hurting world. Secure as sons and daughters, confident in the unconditional love of our Heavenly Daddy, and acutely aware of enemy tactics, we would be an unstoppable force! We would forgive readily and easily, we would not take offence, our churches would not split. God's beloved would not criticise one another; we would not grumble about the church leadership or crave attention. Our love for the lost and unlovely would be outrageous, extravagant and radical. Is this not what we want?

As Brennan Manning has said:

> The greatest single cause of atheism in the world today is Christians, who acknowledge Jesus with their lips, then walk out the door, and deny Him by their lifestyle. That is what an unbelieving world simply finds unbelievable.[20]

So, let's choose to stay very small – let's think of ourselves as four-year-olds. We need to be as dependent on God as a child is on his parents. We don't ever really want to grow up and think that we can 'do life' without His help in every area, every day, all the time, forever. Let's be honest about our failings and misgivings and let's not hide our real selves in the shadows of lies, behind the shallow accolade of performance and competency. Jesus beckons us out into the light of truth, into vulnerability and into intimacy with Abba. He asks us to walk with Him, and in the safety and security of His presence, we will find that we are stronger and more courageous than we thought possible.

---

20 Brennan Manning, quoted in Ben Simpson, 'The Ragamuffin Legacy', *Relevant Magazine*, 16 April 2013. https://www.relevantmagazine.com/faith/ragamuffin-legacy

PAUSE FOR REFLECTION

1. Think about what it means when we read in John 14:6 that Truth is a person – Jesus. What does this look like for you in your relationship with God?

2. The trauma is not really the problem. What we start to believe as a result of the trauma *is*, however, the real problem. Do you identify with this statement from your own experience? How might you process adversity differently next time?

3. Can you identify one or two lies that you already know that you're believing about yourself? Can you see where they may have come from?

4. Would you like to start dismantling the lies? If so, you might like to use this prayer, filling in the blanks depending on your own situation:

I repent of believing the lie that _____. (e.g., I am worthless)

Please forgive me, Lord. I choose to forgive those who have contributed to me believing this lie. _____ (let the Holy Spirit bring to mind those people you need to forgive)

I now choose to break my agreement with this lie, and I break all agreements that I have made with the kingdom of darkness because of this lie.

Now, Father God, what is the truth?
_____ (listen quietly)

I choose to accept, receive and believe the truth that
_____. Amen

After breaking agreement with the lie, over the next 40 days declare the truth aloud, several times a day, especially when the temptation to rehearse the lie presents itself again. This process is simple but powerful. If you are diligent and committed to this, in time, the lie *will* disappear as the truth sinks deep into your heart. Dismantle just one lie at a time; otherwise, it may be too much and potentially discouraging!

A FINAL WORD

*The ache for home lives in all of us, the safe place where we can go
as we are and not be questioned.*
MAYA ANGELOU

It was February 2003. I woke Steve, sleeping beside me, with
a start, the slivers of a dream still touching the edges of my
consciousness. I knew without the shadow of a doubt that God
had spoken to me in the night. 'November 29th'. The words
played on my lips. We would be collecting our baby from
China on November 29th. No doubt about it. However, that
date came and went, and as the months slipped from 2003
into 2004 with no news from China, so the dream faded, and
the promise with it.

Later, we would discover that Phoebe had been born in February
2003, perhaps on the day of the dream. We don't know her

exact birthdate, but her Abba Daddy does. And He kept his promise, of course. The Chinese authorities, unbeknown to them, cooperated with His plans, and she was handed over to us on that very day, clinging to her little red shoes – November 29th – the day she ceased being an orphan and became our daughter, the day she came home.

LIVE FROM REST

In a world obsessed with doing, we are discovering the ancient art of being. Our free Biblically based meditation app and other web based resources are all designed to help fellow pilgrims find and maintain a place of peace, rest and freedom, even amidst the busyness and chaos of 21st century living.

LiveFromRest.com

If you would like to contact Lucinda or to ask her to speak at your church or meeting, please email her:

lucinda@livefromrest.com

The IDENTITY COURSE, based around The Red Thread, is a resource for small groups or individuals. Each of the six sessions includes a 15-20 minute video talk given by Lucinda, with further questions to consider and discuss.

TheRedThread.world

CPSIA information can be obtained
at www.ICGtesting.com
Printed in the USA
LVHW031639170322
713580LV00008B/720